Anna Hazare

The New Revolutionary

Prateeksha M. Tiwari

DIAMOND BOOKS

Publisher : **Diamond Pocket Books (P) Ltd.**
X-30, Okhla Industrial Area, Phase-II
New Delhi - 110020
Phone : 011-40712200
E-mail : sales@dpb.in
Website : www.diamondbook.in

Anna Hazare: The New Revolutionary
By - *Prateeksha M. Tiwari*

Preface

The situation in India today is drastic, and drastic situations require drastic measures. While corruption has existed from time immemorial, recently has probably seen the maximum number of scams being unearthed. And mind you, these are only the scams that have been exposed; there could be a thousand others that have gone unexposed. Earlier, we used to say that corruption exists only in government service; today it has seeped into every single profession. Doctors, lawyers, engineers, the media, and the judiciary--nothing is spared. This is a very dangerous scenario for the country.

In this grim situation Anna Hazare did his fast unto death in support of a stronger Jan Lokpal Bill to fight corruption. He was on fast in front of Jantar Mantar, Delhi and asked the government to create a joint committee with top members from the government and civil society to draft the bill. In support, thousands of people from over 400 cities in India and abroad were sat on similar fasts. People from all backgrounds— students, professionals, activists— were participated in the fast for one cause, a stronger anti-corruption bill.

Most of us don't want to be involved in politics or public affairs. And that is why we choose a government. We only need a fair society to live in. We need good roads to travel, good schools for our children, buses and trains for us to travel. We ask for nothing more. We are decent people only asking for a decent environment to live in. And we deserve it. The current environment has been polluted by corruption and the government has not taken sound steps to curb it. It is high time we realise our duties as citizens and peacefully demand what we deserve.

Most of us see corruption as a problem which is deep rooted in our society and which can't be eradicated. But history has a proof that if committed citizens come together for change, anything is possible. The case of Hong Kong is one fine example. Hong Kong was so corrupt during the 1960s that it was an open secret and a way of life. And the government seemed powerless to do anything about it. But in the early 1970s, one event after another triggered off a storm of public protests and a powerful and independent agency was set up to deal with corruption. An independent commission against corruption was created in 1974 and now Hong Kong is one of the most cleanest and corruption free cities in the world.

At 73 years, Anna did not fast for himself, he was on fast for the future of our country. The media coverage of his fast and other activities was very good. It will surely help in spreading awareness about the issue to the general public.

In this mission of mass movement this book on Anna Hazare may prove useful for readers. How almost an unknown personality like Anna Hazare becomes a celebrity overnight is discussed in this book. Maybe, Anna is unknown to most of us Indian till few months before, but he has a long history of struggles for the common people in his native state, Maharashtra. The corruption scenario in India is also discussed in detail in this book.

—Prateeksha M. Tiwari

Contents

Introduction

Anna Hazare is one of India's well-acclaimed social activists. A former soldier in the Indian army, Anna is well known and respected for upgrading the ecology and economy of the village of Ralegan Siddhi which is located in the drought prone Ahmednagar district of Maharashtra state. The erstwhile barren village has metamorphosed into a unique model of rural development due to its effective water conservation methods, which made the villagers self-sufficient. Earlier, the same village witnessed alcoholism, utter poverty and migration to urban slums. Inspired by Anna Hazare's unique approach of salvaging a hopeless village, the state government has implemented the 'Model Village' scheme as part of its official strategy. Anna Hazare is now synonymous with rural development in India.

Anna Hazare—A new ray of hope

No personality or project incited popular support on such a grand scale after Mahatma Gandhi like Anna Hazare's crusade against corruption.

Anna Hazare conducted the spirited movements, including one for the Right to Information Act, with a photograph of Gandhi on the dais. This is the ritual at all his public platforms.

Like they did with Gandhi, various sections of the society joined the Hazare-led movement. Many leaders and parties joined the escalating movement because they had their own axe to grind.

Background

Anna once contemplated suicide and even wrote a two-page essay on why he wanted to end his life. Anna was not driven to such a pass by circumstances. He wanted to live no more because he was frustrated with life and wanted an answer to the purpose of human existence.

The story goes that one day at the New Delhi Railway Station, he chanced upon a book on Swami Vivekananda. Drawn by Vivekananda's photograph, he is quoted as saying that he read the book and found his answer – that the motive of his life lay in service to his fellow humans.

Today, Anna Hazare is the face of India's fight against corruption. He has taken that fight to the corridors of power and challenged the government at the highest level. People, the common man and well-known personalities alike, are supporting him in the hundreds swelling to the thousands.

For Anna Hazare, it is another battle. And he has fought quite a few, including some as a soldier for 15 years in Indian Army. He enlisted after the 1962 Indo-China war when the government exhorted young men to join the Army.

In 1978, he took voluntary retirement from the 9th Maratha Battalion and returned home to Ralegan Siddhi, a village in

Maharashtra's drought-prone Ahmadnagar. He was 39 years old.

He found farmers back home struggling for survival and their suffering would prompt him to pioneer rainwater conservation that put his little hamlet on the international map as a model village.

The villagers revere him. People of Ralegan says, "Thanks to Anna's agitations, we got a school, electricity and development schemes for farmers."

Anna Hazare's fight against corruption began here. He fought first against corruption that was blocking growth in rural India. His organization—the *Bhrashtachar Virodhi Jan Andolan*. His tool of protest—hunger strikes. And his prime target—politicians.

Anna on his fast unto death at Jantar-Mantar, New Delhi

His weapon is potent. In 1995-96, he forced the Sena-BJP government in Maharashtra to drop two corrupt Cabinet Ministers. In 2003, he forced the Congress-Nationalist Congress Party (NCP) state government to set up an investigation against four ministers.

Maharashtra stalwarts like Sharad Pawar and Bal Thackeray have often called his style of agitation nothing short of "blackmail".

But Anna Hazare has soldiered on relentless from one battle to another in his war against corruption. He fought from the front to have Right to Information (RTI) implemented. He is now fighting for the implementation of the Jan Lokpal Bill, an anti-corruption bill drafted by leading members of civil society that envisages speedy action in corruption cases against everyone, including ministers and senior bureaucrats.

More than 30 years after Anna Hazare started his crusade, as the 72-year-old observed a hunger strike in Delhi against large-scale corruption at the national level, nothing really has changed except the scale of his battle.

Lokpal bills were introduced in 1968, 1971, 1977, 1985, 1989, 1996, 1998, 2001, 2005 and in 2008, yet they were never passed. After a fast by veteran social activist Anna Hazare and widespread protests by citizens across India, the Government of India constituted a 10-member Joint Committee of ministers and civil society activists to draft an effective Jan Lokpal Bill.

Presently 18 states have Lokayukta Acts. However, they are quite ineffective.

❑

1

Know Anna Hazare

Anna Hazare was born as Kisan Baburao Hazare on January 15, 1940 in Bhingar, Ahmednagar district in Maharashtra. This well-known social worker hails from a modest background. His father was an unskilled labourer and they owned five acres of cultivable land. Adverse farming conditions pushed their family into the grip of poverty and in 1952 Anna Hazare moved into his ancestral home in Ralegan Siddhi.

He was brought up by a childless aunt who financed his education in Mumbai but financial instability pushed him into selling flowers for a living and he had to quit studies after class VII. Soon after he was recruited in the Indian Army and trained as a truck driver and was given a posting in Punjab.

His days in the Army were spent in reading books by great philosophers like Swami Vivekananda, Mahatma Gandhi and Acharya Vinoba Bhave. Their thoughts inspired him to devote his life to social work. Two near-fatal mishaps in the 1965 war with Pakistan changed his outlook towards life and seeking voluntary retirement from the army he returned to his ancestral village in 1975.

Ralegan Siddhi, his ancestral village, was then in the grip of drought and poverty. For the betterment of the condition of the village he began to work independently. He used his entire savings for the developmental work of the village. He motivated the villagers into voluntary labour by his Gandhian philosophy. Canals and bundhs were built to hold rainwater which solved the water scarcity problem and also increased irrigational possibilities in the village. Solar panels were fitted all over the village to provide electricity, biogas plants met the people's need for household fuel and wind pumps too were set up.

The village no longer suffered from water scarcity and it has its own grain bank, milk bank and a school. Poverty no longer existed in the village and Anna Hazare himself has successfully motivated the villagers to give up vices like alcohol. Great emphasis is also laid on education, removal of untouchability and collective marriage and the setting up of the Gram Sabha.

Unexpected mass support against corruption

Anna Hazare has truly emerged as 'Anna' or elder brother of his village and his stature today is no less than that of a saint. His immense appeal was proved when he was once arrested in connection with a defamation case in 1998. Following mass public protests, he was immediately released. His achievements have won him many awards like *the Indira Priyadarshini Vrikshamitra Award, the Krishi Bhushan Award, the Padmashri and the Padmabhushan Award.*

He is also one of the leading figures who championed the cause of Right to Information Act in India for his crusade towards fighting corruption in public offices.

❑

2

A Great Social Activist

From a tenacious soldier to a social reformer, Anna Hazare's journey of four decades has been unprecedented in terms of a non-violent yet effective campaign of resurrecting a barren village into an 'ideal village' model and empowering the faceless citizen through pioneering work on Right to Information. His efforts to empower gram panchayats, protect efficient government officers from frequent transfers and fight against the red-tapism in government offices have also received accolades.

His tryst with the army came when many Indian soldiers became martyrs in the Indo-China War of 1962 and the Government of India had appealed to young Indians to join the Indian army. Being passionate about patriotism, he promptly responded to the appeal and joined the Indian Army in 1963. During his 15-year tenure as a soldier, he was posted to several states like Sikkim, Bhutan, Jammu-Kashmir, Assam, Mizoram, Leh and Ladakh and braved challenging weathers.

At times, Hazare used to be frustrated with life and wondered about the very existence of human life. His mind yearned to look out for a solution to this simple and basic question. His frustration reached the peak level and at one particular moment, he also contemplated suicide. For this, he had also penned a two page essay on why he wants to live no more. Fortunately for him, inspiration came from the most unexpected quarters—at the book stall of the railway station of New Delhi, where he was located then. He came across a book of Swami Vivekananda and immediately bought it.

He was inspired by Vivekananda's photograph on the cover. As he started reading the book, he found answers to all his questions, he says. The book revealed to him that the ultimate motive of human life should be service to humanity. Striving for the betterment of common people is equivalent to offering a prayer to the God, he realized.

In the year 1965, Pakistan attacked India and at that time, Hazare was posted at the Khemkaran border. On November 12, 1965, Pakistan launched air attacks on Indian base and all of Hazare's comrades became martyrs. It was a close shave for Hazare as one bullet had passed by his head. Hazare believes this was the turning point of his life as it meant he had a purpose to life.

As already told Anna was greatly influenced by Swami Vivekananda's teachings. It was at that particular moment that Hazare took an oath to dedicate his life in the service of humanity, at the age of 26. He decided not to let go of a life time by being involved merely in earning the daily bread for the family. That's the reason why he pledged to be a bachelor. By then he had completed only three years in the army and so would not be eligible for the pension scheme. In order to be self-sufficient, he continued to be in the army for 12 more years. After that, he opted for voluntary retirement and returned to his native place in Ralegan Siddhi, in the Parner tehsil of Ahmednagar district.

While in the army, Hazare used to visit Ralegan Siddhi for two months every year and used to see the miserable condition of farmers due to water scarcity. Ralegan Siddhi falls in the drought-prone area with a mere 400 to 500 mm of annual rainfall. There were no weirs to retain rainwater. During the month of April and May, water tankers were the only means of drinking water. Almost 80 per cent of the villagers were dependant on other villages for food grains.

Residents used to walk for more than four to six kilometers in search of work and some of them had opted to open country liquor dens as a source of income.

More than 30-35 such dens located in and around the village had tarnished the dignity of the village and marred the social peace. Small scuffles, thefts and physical brawls resulted in loss of civic sense. Morality had reached such a nadir that some of the residents stole wooden logs of the temple of the village deity Yadavbaba to burn the choolah of one of the country liquor outfits.

Anna at his native village—Ralegan Siddhi

Hazare came across the work of one Vilasrao Salunke, a resident of Saswad near Pune who had started a novel project of water management through watershed development in a joint venture with the Gram Panchyat. Hazare visited the project and decided to implement it in Ralegan Siddhi. By keeping an eye on conserving every drop of water and preventing erosion of the fertile soil, he steered the villagers to begin working towards water conservation. At the outset, they completed 48 Nala Bunding work, contour trenches, staggered trenches, gully plugs, meadows development and of forestation of 500 hectares of land. Thereafter, they constructed five RCC weirs and 16 Gabion Weirs.

This resulted in increase in the ground water level. After that, Hazare along with his team worked out the cropping pattern suitable to the quality of soil and the water volume available for farming. This led to increase in the water table by making water available for 1,500 acres of land instead of 300 acres. As a natural sequel, this effort led to yielding of food-grains and the villagers became self-sufficient in terms of food. The table turned turtle– earlier there was no work available for the villagers, now manpower was required to be imported from neighbouring villages.

The changes in the economics brought all the villagers under one roof of unity and people voluntarily contributed in terms of labour and money to build a school, a hostel, a temple and other buildings. Mass marriages, grains bank, dairy, cooperative society, self-help groups for women and youth mandals helped develop the village in all aspects and gave a new face to it.

Hazare opines that proper planning of natural and human resources can result in the betterment of a person, area, village instead of exploiting such resources. He says, "Today we all are exploiting the earthen resources like petrol, diesel, kerosene, coal and water. This can never be termed as perennial development as it is going to lead a state of destruction one day. The sources of energy are limited and hence I am concerned about the next generations. Today many of the villages of almost every state are feeling the brunt of water shortage. Building concrete jungles does not mean development as Gandhiji had rightly said.

Creation of a human idol should be the main objective rather than creating towering buildings. Surely, one needs to live for oneself and the family but simultaneously one owes something to his neighbour, his village and his nation too. For this, one needs an idol who could lead to this goal. Such leadership is not created by power or money but only by virtues like pure thinking, matching action and willingness to sacrifice. It is the thumb rule of farming that when a seed buries itself, it leads to a better yield. In order to get better yield of grains, one single grain needs to burry itself. The society needs such volunteers who are ready to get buried in selfless service for the better future of the society.

Hazare's Ralegan Siddhi became the first role model of an ideal village and has become a tourist spot for many visitors across the nation, since it shows the metamorphoses from the worst village to an ideal village. Visitors include politicians, researchers, social workers and students. Four postgraduate students have completed Ph. D. thesis on Ralegan Siddhi.

Social Life

Anna rightly thought that Development is marred by corruption and started a new venture in 1991 called Bhrashtachar Virodhi Jan Aandolan (BVJA) or public movement against corruption. It was found that some 42 forest officers had duped the state government for crores of rupees through corruption in confederacy. Hazare submitted the evidences to the government but the latter was reluctant to take action against all these officers as one of the ministers of the ruling party was involved in the scam. A distressed Hazare returned the Padmashree Award and also returned the Vriksha Mitra Award.

He further went on an indefinite hunger strike in Alandi on the same issue. Finally, the government woke up from deep slumber and took action against the culprits. Hazare's sustained campaign on this issue had a great effect—six of the ministers were forced to resign and more than 400 officers from different government offices were sent back to home.

Hazare realized that it was not enough to merely take action against fraudulent ministers or officers but to change the entire system that was studded with loopholes. Hence, he campaigned for the Right to Information Act. The state government turned a blind eye towards the pleas in this regard and so he first agitated in the historical Azad Maidan in Mumbai in the year 1997. To create mass public awareness about RTI amongst the youth, Hazare travelled extensively throughout the state. The government kept promising that RTI Act would be made but never raised this issue in the house or the state assembly. Hazare did not relent—he agitated at least ten times.

Finally, again he went on an indefinite hunger strike at Azad Maidan in the last week of July 2003. At last, the President of India signed the draft of the Right to Information Act after his 12-day-long hunger strike and ordered the state government to implement it with effect from 2002. The same draft was considered as the base document for the making of the National Right to Information Act-2005.

After the implementation of the RTI Act-2005, Hazare travelled for more than 12,000 kms across the state creating awareness about the Act. In the second phase, he interacted with more than one lakh college students and also conducted mass public meetings across 24 districts of the state. The third phase included daily 2-3 public meetings in more than 155 tehsil places. In this massive campaign, posters, banners were displayed and more than one lakh booklets of the provisions of the Act were distributed at a nominal price.

This created enough of awareness and people were educated on the issue of rights of citizens.

Hazare deservedly won the coveted Padmashri and then Padmabhushan. Care International of the USA, Transparency International, Seoul (South Korea) also felicitated him. Apart from this, he received awards worth Rs 25 lakh and donated the entire amount for the Swami Vivekananda Kritajnyata Nidhi (social gratitude fund). Out of the two lakh rupees received from the above amount, mass marriages are carried of at least 25-30 poor couples every year.

Hero's welcome for Anna at Ralegan after successful hunger strike

That Hazare has given his life for social betterment is reflected thus: "I do have my home in the village but I have not entered it for the past 35 years. I have implemented schemes costing more than several crores of rupees but I do not have bank balance. Last 12 years I have been working in the field of eradication of corruption. This movement is run entirely by public support without and grants or sponsorships. I appeal for money wherever I go for a public meeting and urge them to contribute generously. The same money I use to carry out my campaigns. The money collected at such public meetings is counted in front of the villagers and my volunteers issue a receipt of the same on the spot."

He further states that, "The movement that we started many years back without a penny in wallet, has spread its wings in all the 33 districts and 252 tehsils of the state. Hence we have been instrumental in offering rights to local bodies like Gramsabha, preventing red-tapism and initiating the law of transfers. This has prevented corruption on a large scale. This has also resulted in offering social justice to the economically backward class. The Union Government keeps on making various schemes for poor people in availing kerosene, LPG and pulses on ration card but the middlemen keep on gulping the subsidies of the same. Our efforts made these necessities available to the poor."

The state government promoted opening of cooperative societies, credit societies and urban banks. Believing in the principles of cooperative sector, the utmost lower class of the society invested their savings with such cooperative societies. However, the directors of such societies devoured the money and failed to pay back the basic amount to the members of the societies. This created havoc and people were duped for crores of rupees and did not have money for the marriages of their daughters or for medical treatment. Hazare agitated for over eight months. The result was that more than Rs 125 crore was recovered from defaulters and the members of such societies heaved a sigh of relief. Recovery of around Rs. 400 crores is in the pipeline.

In the future, the BVJA will work for the decentralisation of power and laws related to the same. Says Hazare, "We have decided to develop centers to create awareness amongst people about government schemes and train activists to know the modus operandi of corruption in each sector. As the state government has decided to set up committees at almost every nodal point like state, district, tehsil and village level with one member on such committee represented by our organisation. We have trained more than 400 volunteers to work on such committees."

❑

3

Anna's Tirade against Corruption

Power Situation during 1985-86 became extremely critical. The farmers were unable to lift water from the wells in spite of its availability due to insufficient voltage to run pumps. The motors were getting burnt due to fluctuations and the crops were getting affected. There was scant response from the govt. in spite of continuous follow-up. On 28 November 1989 Hazare was forced to undertake fast for seeking redressal. After 8 days of his fast, his health deteriorated and was admitted in the civil hospital at Ahmednagar.

As there was, no response in spite of action from his side, the farmers from three tehsils became furious and they started road block agitation. Fearing that if the agitation takes a wrong turn, something untoward might take place, he appealed to the agitators from the hospital bed that they should not resort to unfair means, damage the national property and inflict any harm to the passengers. The agitation should be peaceful. The police authorities did not expect huge participation and there was meager police force available. However, they were proved wrong and more than 10000 men and 1200 women participated in the agitation. The agitators had offered police to take them to jail. However, since enough transport was not available with the police, the police tried to remove the road block. Due to improper treatment meted out to the agitators, there was scuffle between police and the agitators and the police resorted to lathi-charged on agitators. This action on the part of police irritated them and they pelted stones on the police force. Since the situation was going out of control, additional force was called and police opened fire on the agitators in which 4 farmers died on the spot and 7 farmers sustained severe injuries. He felt sad on hearing this news in the hospital. The agitation was meant for awakening the government and there is no harm in carrying out such agitations in democracy. He had decided to end his life during the fast itself, but Senior Officials of the government and even Ministers persuaded him to give up his fast as they feared that if agitation continues, lot many farmers may lose their life and in order to save the life of innocent farmers, he withdrew his fast.

Model Village as contemplated by Gandhiji was brought in reality by Anna at Ralegan Siddhi by his dedication. Late Achyutrao Patwardhan, the great freedom fighter, suggested to the government of Maharashtra that to commemorate the golden jubilee of Bharat Chhodo Andolan, it would be most befitting to create model villages like Ralegan Siddhi in every tehsil of the state. The government accepted this suggestion and declared to implement Adarsh Gaon Yojana. The Government entrusted this responsibility to him and Adarsh Gaon Yojana was started under his leadership. He travelled whole of Maharashtra and selected 300 villages to implement this scheme. While working in this scheme he realised that development is getting hampered due to planned corruption in Government machinery and he decided to fight against this corruption. He gave evidence against two ministers who had amassed wealth disproportionate to their income. However since the Government was passive about this he started agitation and undertook fast for 10 days. Chief Minister intervened and he deleted these two ministers from ministry and appointed an Inquiry Commission. The Commission held both the ministers guilty but to save them the Governmentt appointed another commission who discharged them from the allegations. Though the ministers were discharged from the allegations, they had to lose their ministership which is the success of Hazare's agitation.

A modern day Mahatma

He wanted to complete his jail term but to give respect to the public feelings he accepted his release. Once Gandhiji had told the court that if court feels that his actions for the freedom of the country are considered as anti government activities he was willing to undergo any punishment. Similarly Hazare did not give bond to the court and accepted punishment. He did not prefer any appeal against the court order immediately but due to public pressure he later made an appeal which was upheld by the Higher Court and rejected the suit of minister. Hazare asked the Government to conduct the inquiry against the minister which is still on.

In the regime of coalition Government of Congress and National Congress Party, he had forwarded evidence of corruption about four ministers and had asked the Government to conduct inquiry. One of the ministers had made allegations about corruption in the institutions in which he was associated. Since there was no action from the Govt. he undertook fast for 9 days in August 2003 at Azad Maidan. The minister concerned also started agitation at Azad Maidan in Mumbai. At last the Government relented and Retired Supreme Court Judge P.B. Sawant was appointed to conduct the inquiry. The commission conducted the inquiry and sent its report to Government on 22nd February.

In the report, the commission had observed ministers guilty and had held Hazare also guilty for irregularities but not a single charge of corruption was proved against him. Hazare has offered the Government that it should take action against him as well as the ministers based on the findings of the enquiry commissions. Though Government has not taken any action on the Commission's report three ministers had to go and this is a big achievement of his agitation against corruption.

He felt that corruption will not stop merely by taking action against a few officers and ministers and it is necessary that a change should be brought about in the system. He believes that unless decentralisation of power takes place, the system will not change. In order to bring change in the system he felt that information should be made available to people regarding Government's actions which was not being provided to people on the ground of secrecy. Here again he decided to follow Gandhiji's path and started Maun Vrat and later fast unto death. This brought pressure on the Government and both the Central as well as State Governments have enacted Right to Information Act. His whole life and work is based on Gandhian philosophy.

❑

4

Corruption in India

"Power tends to corrupt, and absolute power corrupts absolutely."•

It is not easy to define corruption. But in a narrow sense, corruption is mostly concerned with bribery and it takes several forms. Corruption is a global phenomenon and it is omnipresent. Corruption has progressively increased and is now rampant in our society.

Indians' anger over rising corruption has reached feverish levels. What people are calling a "season of scams" includes the alleged theft of billions by officials behind last year's Commonwealth games in Delhi; $40 billion in revenues lost from the crooked sale of 2G telecoms licences; and over $40 billion stolen in Uttar Pradesh alone from schemes subsidising food and fuel for the poor. Foreign businessmen, who have slashed investment over the past year, rank graft as their biggest headache behind appalling infrastructure. Now India's anti-corruption chief has been forced out over corruption.

National Scenario

Corruption in India is a consequence of the nexus between bureaucracy, politics and criminals. India is now no longer considered a soft state. It has now become a consideration state where everything can be had for a consideration. Today, the number of ministers with an honest image can be counted on fingers. At one time, bribe was paid for getting wrong things done but now bribe is paid for getting right things done at right time.

Indian administration is tainted with scandals. India is among top countries where corruption is rampant, according to the Corruption Perception Index Report released by Transparency International India. Corruption in India leads to promotion not prison. It is very difficult to catch 'big sharks'. Corruption in India has wings not wheels. As nation grows, the corrupt also grows to invent new methods of cheating the government and public.

What Causes Corruption?

The causes of corruption are many and complex. Following are some of the causes of corruption.

- Emergence of political elite who believe in interest-oriented rather than nation-oriented programmes and policies.
- Artificial scarcity created by the people with malevolent intentions wrecks the fabric of the economy.
- Corruption is caused as well as increased because of the change in the value system and ethical qualities of men who administer. The old ideals of morality, service and honesty are regarded as an achronistic.
- Tolerance of people towards corruption, complete lack of intense public outcry against corruption and the absence of strong public forum to oppose corruption allow corruption to reign over people.
- Vast size of population coupled with widespread illiteracy and the poor economic infrastructure lead to endemic corruption in public life.

- In a highly inflationary economy, low salaries of government officials compel them to resort to the road of corruption. Graduates from IIMs with no experience draw a far handsome salary than what government secretaries draw.
- Complex laws and procedures alienate common people to ask for any help from government.
- Election time is a time when corruption is at its peak level. Big industrialist fund politicians to meet high cost of election and ultimately to seek personal favour. Bribery to politicians buys influence, and bribery by politicians buys votes. In order to get elected, politicians bribe poor illiterate people, who are slogging for two times' meal.

Measures to Combat Corruption

Is it possible to eradicate corruption from our society? Corruption is a cancer, which every Indian must strive to cure. Many new leaders when come into power declare their determination to eradicate corruption but soon they themselves become corrupt and start amassing huge wealth.

There are many myths about corruption, which have to be exploded if we really want to combat it. Some of these myths are: Corruption is a way of life and nothing can be done about it. Only people from underdeveloped or developing countries are prone to corruption. We will have to guard against all these crude fallacies while planning measures to fight corruption.

- Foolproof laws should be made so that there is no room for discretion for politicians and bureaucrats. The role of the politician should be minimized. Application of the evolved policies should be left in the hands of independent commission or authority in each area of public interest. Decision of the commission or authority should be challengeable only in the courts.

- Cooperation of the people has to be obtained for successfully containing corruption. People should have a right to recall the elected representatives if they see them becoming indifferent to the electorate.

- Funding of elections is at the core of political corruption. Electoral reforms are crucial in this regard. Several reforms like: State funding of election expenses for candidates; strict enforcement of statutory requirements like holding in-party elections, making political parties get their accounts audited regularly and filing income-tax returns; denying persons with criminal records a chance to contest elections, should be brought in.

- Responsiveness, accountability and transparency are a must for a clean system. Bureaucracy, the backbone of good governance, should be made more citizen friendly, accountable, ethical and transparent.

- More and more courts should be opened for speedy and inexpensive justice so that cases don't linger in courts for years and justice is delivered on time.
- Local bodies, Independent of the government, like Lokpals, Lok Adalats, CVCs and Vigilance Commissions should be formed to provide speedy justice with low expenses.
- A new Fundamental Right *viz.* Right to Information should be introduced, which will empower the citizens to ask for the information they want. Barring some confidential information, which concerns national and international security, other information should be made available to general public as and when required. Stringent actions against corrupt officials will certainly have a deterrent impact.

Conclusion

Corruption is an intractable problem. It is like diabetes, can only be controlled, but not totally eliminated. It may not be possible to root out corruption completely at all levels but it is possible to contain it within tolerable limits. Honest and dedicated persons in public life, control over electoral expenses could be the most important prescriptions to combat corruption. Corruption has a corrosive impact on our economy. It worsens our image in international market and leads to loss of overseas opportunities. Corruption is a global problem that all countries of the world have to confront, solutions, however, can only be home grown. We have tolerated corruption for so long. The time has now come to root it out from its roots.

❑

5

Scam after Scam

Corruption in India is not a secret from anyone, as it is prevalent from private to the public sector and almost everyone in the system is part of the misdoings. However, the extent to which the Indian public sector employees and politicians have taken corruption is drastic.

The damage caused by corruption to the Indian state exchequer is immense, with Indians hoarding $1,456 billion in black money at Swiss banks. Apart from the amounts of black money on foreign shores, the controversies revolving around the Commonwealth Games had led to the country not only suffering from financial leaks, but the irresponsibility of the top officials also damaged the country's reputation abroad and had almost jeopardized the games, which were being touted as the biggest sporting event on Indian soil.

Another leader, who has cheated the Indian public, is none other than the former Telecom Minister A. Raja, the man who turned his back on his countrymen by the sale of 2G spectrum at a minimal cost and caused damages to the country amounting to Rs. 1.76 lakh crores. A cabinet minister stooping so low for selfish gains is not just pathetic but aggravating, no wonder people are angry and are baffled about how such a thing could happen, when the system has been made to prevent such discrepancies.

This disease of corruption is so widespread in the country that it has not spared the men of honour in the armed forces, with the names of some top defence officers in India being named in a scam involving a housing society in Mumbai.

A part from Indians being well informed about the so-called intricacies of the system, India has also earned a few special titles regarding corruption. The nation has been ranked 1st in a list of 30 countries related to the readiness of companies to pay bribes for business contracts, in both, the public and the private sector.

Though India has been touted to be one of the fastest growing nations in the world, it is not surprising to see that the country at the same time is suffering from an epidemic known as corruption..

The country could very well be defined as a failed administrative state, as the country has been ranked 97th out of 146 countries, in a Failed States Index by Foreign Policy in Washington. India also has the distinction of being ranked 70th in a list of 183 countries by Transparency International, who look into the cleanliness of businesses in the country.

Though bribery has been part of the nation since its heydays, the only cause of concern is that India's economy is suffering immensely because of these corrupt men, who never fail to make a buck for themselves by stealing the hard earned money of Indian people from the state exchequer. Let's hope the so-called self proclaimed world's 3rd largest economy does not lose out on its potential because of corrupt politicians and bureaucrats.

❑

6

Major Scams in India

This is the season of scams and the biggest ever corruption cases in India have been unearthed more recently. So, we decided to dig deep to see which scams were the biggest and most damaging to the country and its citizens alike.

In our daily life, most of us must have been a witness to or a victim of the corruption thriving in some or the other part of the country. It could be in the form of a taxi-driver manipulating the meter to jack-up the reading or a government officer taking bribe to transfer promptly your file to the next department or even yourself offering bribe to a traffic police on breaking a signal.

An average Indian citizen is hard working and diligent, but it is the people in charge of the system or with whom the power rests, that act as a cancer spreading the venom, slowing down progress and what all not. But, somewhere down the line, we ourselves are responsible for allowing and being taken for a ride by these people, aren't we?

However, it is during a multi-thousand crore scam, that a tax-payer actually realizes the heartburn of being cheated from his valued contribution of funds towards the development and well-being of the nation. But, that's what a scam, be it big or small, means—the act of swindling by some fraudulent scheme or action.

Our book is mainly focused on corruption, so it is relevant here to tell readers about some famous scams taken place in India.

Mundhra Scandal

The Mundhra scandal involved the then finance minister T.T. Krishnamachari, who pressured the government-owned Life Insurance Corporation of India into bailing out Haridas Mundhra, a Calcutta-based industrialist, by buying shares worth Rs 1.24 crore in six companies owned by him. LIC did so dutifully, bypassing its own investment committee. Mundhra was swindling the companies and, simultaneously, rigging up their stock prices to camouflage his fraud. TTK, as the minister was popularly known, least expected that this shady deal would be exposed by the PM's own son-in-law.

Although Feroze Gandhi belonged to the ruling party, he did not hesitate to speak out against the government because he argued that corruption in high places was a betrayal of the ideals of the newly independent nation. To be fair to Pandit Nehru, he quickly appointed a one-man commission headed by Justice M.C. Chagla, one of the most respected legal luminaries of the time.

The speedy and transparent manner in which Chagla conducted the inquiry—it was all over, and the guilty were punished, in less than two years—ought to have been a model for all such probes. All its hearings were public and the proceedings were aired on loudspeakers. Mundhra was sentenced to 22 years in prison, and TTK lost his job.

Fodder Scam

Fodder Scam is a scam related to Animal Husbandry Department of Government of Bihar in which irregularities of nearly Rs 950 crores were detected. The scam was unearthed in 1996 during the regime of chief Minister Lalu Prasad Yadav, but it goes back to 1980s and is believed to have started during tenure of Jagannath Mishra Lalu had ordered probe into these massive irregularities in accounts by constituting a committee. However motives of these people were questioned by a Public Interest Litigation and Supreme Court of India handed over the case to CBI. Many people who were in this probe committee themselves became accused. Charges were filed against Lalu Yadav too and later on Jagannath Mishra was also framed.

CBI filed 69 different cases related to this scam. 31 of which has been in Jharkhand and remaining in Bihar. The charges were framed under: Sections 420 and 120 (b) of the Indian Penal Code and Section 13 (b) of the Prevention of Corruption Act. There are a total of 76 accused, of whom three have died and three turned state witnesses.

It was only after Special Investigation Team (SIT) under U.N. Biswas that investigation started at a brisk rate. Soon many heads started rolling and Lalu Yadav and members of his party had to lose their ministerial berths both at centre and state facing corruption charges.

Bofors Scandal

The Bofors Scandal was a major corruption scandal in India in the 1980s; the then Prime Minister Rajiv Gandhi and several others were accused of receiving kickbacks from Bofors AB for winning a bid to supply India's 155 mm field howitzer. The scale of the corruption was far worse than any that India had seen before, and directly led to the defeat of Rajiv Gandhi's ruling Indian National Congress party in the November 1989 general elections. The case came to light during Vishwanath Pratap Singh's tenure as defence minister.

The name of the middleman associated with the scandal was Ottavio Quattrocchi, an Italian businessman who represented the petrochemicals firm Snamprogetti. Quattrocchi was close to the family of Prime Minister Rajiv Gandhi and emerged as a powerful broker in the '80s between big business and the Indian government.

Even while the case was being investigated, Rajiv Gandhi was assassinated on May 21, 1991 during his election campaign.

In 1997, the Swiss banks released some 500 documents after years of legal wrangling and the Central Bureau of Investigation filed a case against Quattrocchi, Win Chadha, also naming Rajiv Gandhi, the defence secretary and a number of others. Several attempts to extradite Quattrocchi failed.

Meanwhile, on February 5, 2004 Delhi High Court quashed the charges of bribery against Rajiv Gandhi and others, but the case is still being tried on charges of cheating, causing wrongful loss to the Government, etc. Win Chadha also died.

On May 31, 2005, the High court of Delhi dismissed the Bofors case allegations against the British business brothers, Srichand, Gopichand and Prakash Hinduja.

In December 2005, the B. Datta, the additional solicitor general of India, acting on behalf of the Indian Government and the CBI, requested the British Government that two British bank accounts of Ottavio Quattrocchi be de-frozen on the grounds of insufficient evidence to link these accounts to the Bofors payoff. The two accounts, containing • 3 million and $1 million, had been frozen in 2003 by a high court order by request of the Indian government.

The accounts were de-frozen on January 11, 2006. On January 16, the Indian Supreme Court directed the Indian government to ensure that Ottavio Quattrocchi did not withdraw money from the two bank accounts in London. The CBI (Central Bureau Of Investigation) on January 23, 2006 admitted that roughly Rs 21 crore in the two accounts have already been withdrawn. The British Government released the funds based on a request by the Indian Government. At the time a Congress-led alliance was in power, and Sonia Gandhi, as President of the Congress Party, faced considerable criticism for this sudden volte face by the Indian government.

However, on January 16, 2006, CBI claimed in an affidavit filed before the Supreme Court that they were still pursuing extradition orders for Quattrocchi. The Interpol, at the request of the CBI, has a long standing red corner notice to arrest Quattrocchi.

Quattrocchi was detained in Argentina on 6 February 2007, but the news of his detention was released by the CBI only on 23 February, stoking claims that it may have been suppressed by the ruling Congress government because of state elections.

Quattrocchi has been released by Argentinian police.

Harshad Mehta Scam

In April 1992, the Indian stock market crashed, and Harshad Mehta, the person who was all along considered as the architect of the bull run was blamed for the crash. It transpired that he had manipulated the Indian banking systems to siphon off the funds from the banking system, and used the liquidity to build large positions in a select group of stocks. When the scam broke out, he was called upon by the banks and the financial institutions to return the funds, which in turn set into motion a chain reaction, necessitating liquidating and exiting from the positions which he had built in various stocks. The panic reaction ensued, and the stock market reacted and crashed within days. He was arrested on June 5, 1992 for his role in the scam.

As an aftermath of the shockwaves which engulfed the Indian financial sector, a number of people holding key positions in the India's financial sector were adversely affected, which included arrest and sacking of K.M. Margabandhu, then CMD of the UCO Bank; removal from office of V. Mahadevan, one of the Managing Directors of India's largest bank, the State Bank of India.

The Central Bureau of Investigation which is India's premier investigative agency, was entrusted with the task of deciphering the modus operandi and the ramifications of the scam. Harshad Mehta was arrested and investigations continued for a decade. During his judicial custody, while he was in Thane Prison, Mumbai, he complained of chest pain, and was moved to a hospital, where he died on 31st December 2001.

Lakhubhai Pathak Cheating Scandal

Lakhubhai Pathak, an Indian businessman living in England alleged that Chandraswami and K.N. Aggarwal alias Mamaji, along with Narsimha Rao, cheated him out of $100,000. The amount was given for an express promise for allowing supplies of paper pulp in India, and Pathak alleged that he spent an additional $30,000 entertaining Chandraswami and his secretary. Rao and Chandraswami were acquitted of the charges in 2003, due to lack of evidence. Despite this, it remained a large black mark.

Ketan Parekh Scandal

Companies when raising money from the stock market rope in brokers to back them in raising the share price. Ketan Parekh formed a network of brokers from smaller exchanges like the Allahabad Stock Exchange and the Calcutta Stock Exchange. Ketan also used benami share purchase in the name of poor people living in the shanty towns of Mumbai. Ketan's rise to fame occurred at the same time as the worldwide dot-com boom (1999-2000) and he relied primarily on the shares of ten companies for his dealings (now known infamously as the K-10 scrips).

Ketan had large borrowings from Global Trust Bank, whose shares he was ramping up (so that he could get a good deal at the time of its merger with UTI Bank) –he got Rs 250 crore loan from Global Trust Bank, though Global Trust's chairman Ramesh Gelli (who was later asked to quit) repeatedly said that lending to Ketan was less than Rs 100 crore in keeping with Reserve Bank of India norms. Ketan and his associates got another Rs 1,000 crore from the

Madhavpura Mercantile Co-operative Bank despite the fact that RBI regulations ruled that the maximum a broker could have got as a loan was Rs 15 crore.

Thus, Ketan's modus operandi was clearly to ramp up shares of select firms in collusion with the promoters-ironically, during the Ketan cleanup, SEBI concluded a 3-year old case where Harshad Mehta colluded with the managements of BPL, Sterlite and Videocon to ramp up their shares with money provided by these managements-and to get funding from them to do this. In the current Ketan case, SEBI has found prima facie evidence of price rigging in the scrips of Global Trust Bank, Zee Telefilms, HFCL, Lupin Laboratories, Aftek Infosys and Padmini Polymer.

Now with the prices of select shares constantly going up,thanks largely to this rigging,innocent investors who bought such shares thinking the market as genuine,were at loss. Soon after discovery of this scam,the prices of these stocks came down to the fraction of the values at which they were bought. The scam burst and the rigged shares came down so heavily that quite a few people in India lost their savings. Some banks including Bank of India lost money heavily.

At this time a group of traders (known as the bear cartel-Shankar Sharma, Anand Rathi, Nirmal Bang) relied on the global meltdown of stocks to make their profits. Bears sell stocks at high prices and buyback at low prices. At the time of the year 2000 Financial Budget this cartel placed sell orders on the K-10 stocks and crushed their inflated prices. All the borrowing of Ketan's could not rescue his scrips. The Global Trust Bank and the Madhavpura Cooperative went bust because the money they had lent to Ketan had sunk with his K-10 stocks.

The information which was furnished by the Reserve Bank of India to the Joint Parliamentary Committee (JPC),during the investigation of the scam revealed that Financial institutions like Industrial Development Bank of India (IDBI

Bank) and Industrial Finance Corporation of India (IFCI) had extended loans of Rs 1,400-odd crore to companies known to be close to broker Ketan Parekh.

Ketan Parekh was later arrested on December 2, 2002 in Kolkata.

Abdul Karim Telgi Scam

The Telgi case is another big scam that rocked India. The fake stamp racket involving Abdul Karim Telgi was exposed in 2000. The loss is estimated to be Rs 171.33 crore (Rs 1.71 billion), it was initially pegged to be Rs 30,000 crore (Rs 300 bilion), which was later clarified by the CBI as an exaggerated figure.In 1994, Abdul Karim Telgi acquired a stamp paper license from the Indian government and began printing fake stamp papers.

Abdul Karim Telgi is a convicted-counterfeiter from India. He earned money to the tune of several billion US dollars by printing counterfeit stamp paper in India. The scale of his operation and scam can only be matched by the stock market scam of the early 1990s in India done by late Big Bull Harshad Mehta.

Born to an employee of Indian Railways in 1961, Telgi was left to fend for himself at an early age after his father's death. He paid for his own education at Sarvodaya Vidyalaya, an English medium school, by selling fruit and vegetables on trains. He completed his B.Com from a Belgaum college. After this, he moved to Saudi Arabia. Seven years later, he returned to India and began to work as a travel agent.

Telgi was arrested in 1991 by Mumbai police for fraud. During his subsequent prison sentence, he reportedly learned the art of forgery from an expert. He was released and, in 1994, acquired a stamp paper licence from the Government of India.

Telgi bribed to get into the government security press in Nashik and bought special machines to print fake stamp papers. Telgi's network spread across 13 states involving 176 offices, 1,000 employees and 123 bank accounts in 18 cities.

He began printing fake stamp paper. He appointed 300 people as agents who sold the fakes to bulk purchasers, including banks, FIs, insurance companies, and share-broking firms. His monthly profits have been estimated nearly Rs 202 crore. The size of the scam was estimated to be more than 43,000 Cr Rupees.

2G Spectrum Scam

We have had a number of scams in India; but none bigger than the scam involving the process of allocating unified access service licenses. At the heart of this Rs.1.76-lakh crore worth of scam is that the former Telecom Minister, A. Raja – who according to the CAG, has evaded norms at every level as he carried out the dubious 2G license awards in 2008 at a throw-away price which were pegged at 2001 prices.

From the time allegations of misappropriation during the bidding for allocation of 2G spectrum surfaced, till Telecom Minister, A Raja's ouster, high drama charged both politics in Delhi and Tamil Nadu. So what exactly is the Spectrum Scam that led to all this?

What is Spectrum Scam?

- 2G licenses issued to private telecom players at throwaway prices in 2008
- CAG: Spectrum scam has cost the government Rs. 1.76 lakh crore
- CAG: Rules and procedures flouted while issuing licenses

Cheap Telecom Licenses

- Entry fee for spectrum licenses in 2008 pegged at 2001 prices
- Mobile subscriber base had shot up to 350 million in 2008 from 4 million in 2001

No Procedures Followed

- Rules changed after the game had begun
- Cut-off date for applications advanced by a week
- Licenses issued on a first-come-first-served basis
- No proper auction process followed, no bids invited
- Raja ignored advice of TRAI, Law Ministry, Finance Ministry
- TRAI had recommended auctioning of spectrum at market rates

Favouritism, Corporates Encash Premium

- Unitech, Swan Telecom got licenses without any prior telecom experience
- Swan Telecom given license even though it did not meet eligibility criteria
- Swan got license for Rs. 1537 crore, sold 45% stake to Etisalat for Rs. 4200 crore
- Unitech Wireless got license for Rs. 1661 crore, sold 60% stake for Rs. 6200 crore
- All nine companies paid DoT only Rs. 10,772 crore for 2G licences

Chargesheet & Arrests in 2G scam

Filing its first chargesheet in the 2G spectrum allocation scam in a special court, the CBI indicted the former Union Telecom Minister, A. Raja for allegedly conspiring with senior bureaucrats and industrialists to illegally manipulate this second generation spectrum allocation during 2007-08 and cause a loss of Rs 30,984 crore to the national exchequer.

Besides Raja and eight other persons, including bureaucrats and corporate big-wigs, three companies – Anil Ambani-headed ADAG's Reliance Telecom, Unitech Wireless and Swan Telecom – were named as accused in the 2G scam in the CBI's chargesheet.

The CBI has slapped a range of charges, including cheating, forgery, corruption and criminal conspiracy, on them.

Raja has been charged with 'manipulating' procedures like advancing the cut-off date for 2G telecom licences' applications in conspiracy with officials and industrialists by privately conveying to them the rescheduled date and grant of licences to ineligible applicants. He has been charged with cheating, forgery and abuse of official position under the provisions of Indian Penal Code and Prevention of Corruption Act.

The CBI alleged that Raja, the former telecom secretary Siddharth Behura, Raja's personal secretary R.K. Chandolia, Swan Telecom's promoter Shahid Usman Balwa, and the Unitech Wireless' Managing Director, Sanjay Chandra, entered into a conspiracy for manipulating the procedure for allocation of spectrum with the aim of favouring companies like Swan Telecom and Unitech Group.

The agency also dealt with the criminality involved in the decision-taking mechanism by Raja and officials of the Department of Telecom (DoT) with regard to first-come-first-served (FCFS) policy, allowing dual technology to telecom companies and granting licences to ineligible companies and loss caused to the national exchequer.

The charge-sheet, running into about 80,000 pages and brought in seven steel trunks, was filed before the CBI judge Mr O.P. Saini in a special court constituted exclusively to try the 2G scam case that is being monitored by the Supreme Court.

The Attorney General G.E. Vahanvati and the corporate lobbyist Niira Radia have been named among 125 witnesses in the case.

The CBI will file the supplementary chargesheet soon and is likely to complete its probe by 31st May in the politically-sensitive 2 G case.

Raja, Chandolia, Behura and Shahid Balwa were arrested earlier by the CBI and are in jail now. Later, Swan Telecom Director Vinod Goenka, Unitech Wireless (Tamil Nadu) Ltd Managing Director Sanjay Chandra, and three top officials of Reliance ADA Group—Gautam Doshi, Surendra Pipara and Hari Nair were arrested and sent to jail.

The CBI said the gamut of offences were five-fold including the advancing of cut-off date for receiving applications for the 2G licences to help accused companies Swan Telecom and Unitech.

According to CBI counsel, "Investigation has disclosed that Swan Telecom was an associate of Reliance ADA Group. Both the companies had no business history and were activated solely for the purpose of applying for UAS license in 13 circles. The Reliance Telecom did not have GSM spectrum for these circles and it had already applied for dual technology spectrum for these circles. Investigation has revealed that the accused Nair, Doshi and Pipara had wrongly represented themselves as the Directors and other high-ranking officials of the Swan Telecom.

The CBI also told the court that Kalaignar TV Pvt Ltd, Cineyug Films, Green House Pvt Ltd and Kusegaon Fruits and Vegetables Pvt Ltd are also under its scrutiny and investigation is under way.

Kalaignar TV's shares are held by the Tamil Nadu Chief Minister, M. Karunanidhi's daughter and DMK MP, Kanimozhi, his wife Dayaluammal, and the TV's MD

Sharad Kumar in the ration of 20 %, 60%, and 20% respectively. The CBI has alleged that about Rs 200 crore money connected with the 2G scam had been transferred from Shahid Balwa-promoted Swan Telecom to Kalaignar TV through Cineyug Films and Kusegaon Fruits and Vegetables Pvt Ltd.

CBI is also investigating Kaliagnar TV, Asif Balwa and Rajiv Aggarwal, who are the directors of Kusegaon Fruits and Vegetables, and Cineyug and Green House Promoters. They are likely to be named in the supplementary charge-sheet that will be submitted later on.

Asif Balwa is said to be Shahid Balwa's cousin. Green House Promoters' Sadiq Batcha, a close Raja aide, was alleged to have committed suicide in his Chennai residence last month under mysterious circumstances.

The CBI is set to inquire into his death. Asif and Rajiv were recently arrested by the CBI.

The CBI has mentioned 654 documents and names of 125 witnesses in the voluminous 80,000 pages charge-sheet. Among the 125 witnesses listed in the charge-sheet are over 50 senior government officials, most of them belonging to the telecom ministry.

The CBI had earlier informed the Supreme Court that Swan Telecom and Loop Telecom were used as front companies by Relience Telecom and Essar, who have stakes in Vodafone, to get 2G Spectrum illegally during Mr Raja's tenure.

The 2G spectrum scam is widely dubbed as the biggest corruption scam of independent India. The Comptroller and Auditor-General (CAG) of India has pegged the "presumptive" loss due to this scam at a staggering Rs 1.76 lakh crore.

❑

7

Anti Corruption System Needs a Change

Why is it that no one goes to jail in our country despite indulging in corruption? This is because we have completely rotten anti-corruption laws and anti-corruption agencies that it is almost impossible for the corrupt to be penalized.

Justice Santosh Hegde (former Supreme Court Judge and present Lokayukta of Karnataka), Prashant Bhushan (Supreme Court Lawyer) and Arvind Kejriwal (Social Activist) have together drafted a strong anti-corruption law called Jan Lokpal Bill which requires that investigations into any case should be completed within a year and the trial should get over in the next one year so that a corrupt person goes to jail within two years of complaint and his ill gotten wealth is confiscated.

Lokpal Bill has been introduced eight times in Parliament since 1968. All the eight versions have been very weak. Even these weak versions have not been passed so far because Lokpal Bill seeks to investigate politicians. 'The latest draft of Lokpal Bill prepared by the present UPA government is complete eyewash. Rather than strengthen anti-corruption systems, it demolishes whatever exists in the name of anti-corruption systems today. It seeks to completely insulate politicians from any kind of action against them' – This is the view of many social activist who joined the movement of Anna Hazare against corruption.

Deficiencies in Present System

At central Government level, there is Central Vigilance Commission, Departmental vigilance and CBI. CVC and Departmental vigilance deal with vigilance (disciplinary proceedings) aspect of a corruption case and CBI deals with criminal aspect of that case.

Central Vigilance Commission (CVC)

CVC is the apex body for all vigilance cases in Government of India.

- However, it does not have adequate resources commensurate with the large number of complaints that it receives. CVC is a very small set up with a staff strength less than 200. It is supposed to check corruption in more than 1500 central government departments and ministries, some of them being as big as Central Excise, Railways, Income Tax etc. Therefore, it has to depend on the vigilance wings of respective departments and forwards most of the complaints for inquiry and report to them. While it monitors the progress of these complaints, there is delay and the complainants are often disturbed by this. It directly enquires into a few complaints on its own, especially when it suspects motivated delays or where senior officials could be implicated. But given the constraints of manpower, such number is really small.

- CVC is merely an advisory body. Central Government Departments seek CVC's advice on various corruption cases. However, they are free to accept or reject CVC's advice. Even in those cases, which are directly enquired into by the CVC, it can only advise government. CVC mentions these cases of non-acceptance in its monthly reports and the Annual

Report to Parliament. But these are not much in focus in Parliamentary debates or by the media.

- Experience shows that CVC's advice to initiate prosecution is rarely accepted and whenever CVC advised major penalty, it was reduced to minor penalty. Therefore, CVC can hardly be treated as an effective deterrent against corruption.

- CVC cannot direct CBI to initiate enquiries against any officer of the level of Joint Secretary and above on its own. The CBI has to seek the permission of that department, which obviously would not be granted if the senior officers of that department are involved and they could delay the case or see to it that permission would not be granted.

- CVC does not have powers to register criminal case. It deals only with vigilance or disciplinary matters.

  It does not have powers over politicians. If there is an involvement of a politician in any case, CVC could at best bring it to the notice of the Government. There are several cases of serious corruption in which officials and political executive are involved together.

- It does not have any direct powers over departmental vigilance wings. Often it is seen that CVC forwards a complaint to a department and then keeps sending reminders to them to enquire and send report. Many a times, the departments just do not comply. CVC does not have any really effective powers over them to seek compliance of its orders.

- CVC does not have administrative control over officials in vigilance wings of various central government departments to which it forwards corruption complaints. Though the government does consult CVC before appointing the Chief Vigilance Officers of various departments, however, the final decision lies with the government. Also, the officials below CVO are appointed/transferred by that department only. Only in exceptional cases, if the CVO chooses to bring it to the notice of CVC, CVC could bring pressure on the Department to revoke orders but again such recommendations are not binding.

- Appointments to CVC are directly under the control of ruling political party, though the leader of the opposition is a member of the committee to select CVC and VCs. But the Committee only considers names put up before it and that is decided by the Government. The appointments are opaque.

- CVC Act gives supervisory powers to CVC over CBI. However, these supervisory powers have remained ineffective. CVC does not have the power to call for any file from CBI or to direct them to do any case in a particular manner. Besides, CBI is under administrative control of DOPT rather than CVC.

- Therefore, though CVC is relatively independent in its functioning, it neither has resources nor powers to enquire and take action on complaints of corruption in a manner that meets the expectations of people or act as an effective deterrence against corruption.

Departmental Vigilance Wings

Each Department has a vigilance wing, which is manned by officials from the same department (barring a few which have an outsider as Chief Vigilance Officer. However, all the officers under him belong to the same department).

- Since the officers in the vigilance wing of a department are from the same department and they can be posted to any position in that department anytime, it is practically impossible for them to be independent and objective while inquiring into complaints against their colleagues and seniors. If a complaint is received against a senior officer, it is impossible to enquire into that complaint because an officer who is in vigilance today might get posted under that senior officer some time in future.

- In some departments, especially in the Ministries , some officials double up as vigilance officials. It means that an existing official is given additional duty of vigilance also. So, if some citizen complaints against that officer, the complaint is expected to be enquired into by the same officer. Even if someone complaints against that officer to the CVC or to the Head of that Department or to any other authority, the complaint is forwarded by all these agencies and it finally lands up in his own lap to enquire against himself. Even if he recuses himself from such inquiries , still they have to be handled by those who otherwise report to him. There are indeed examples of such absurdity.
- There have been instances of the officials posted in vigilance wing by that department having had a very corrupt past. While in vigilance, they try to scuttle all cases against themselves. They also turn vigilance wing into a hub of corruption, where cases are closed for consideration.
- Departmental vigilance does not investigate into criminal aspect of any case. It does not have the powers to register an FIR.
- They also do not have any powers against politicians.
- Since the vigilance wing is directly under the control of the Head of that Department, it is practically

impossible for them to enquire against senior officials of that department.

- Therefore, the vigilance wing of any department is seen to soft-pedal on genuine complaints or used to enquire against 'inconvenient' officers.

Central Bureau of Investigation (CBI)

CBI has powers of a police station to investigate and register FIR. It can investigate any case related to a Central Government department on its own or any case referred to it by any state government or any court.

- CBI is overburdened and does not accept cases even where amount of defalcation is alleged to be around Rs 1 crore.
- CBI is directly under the administrative control of Central Government.
- So, if a complaint pertains to any minister or politician who is part of a ruling coalition or a bureaucrat who is close to them, CBI's credibility has suffered and there is increasing public perception that it cannot do a fair investigation and that it is influenced to scuttle these cases.
- Again, because CBI is directly under the control of Central Government, CBI is perceived to have been often used to settle scores against inconvenient politicians.

Therefore, if a citizen wants to make a complaint about corruption by a politician or an official in the Central Government, there isn't a single anti-corruption agency which is effective and independent of the government, whose wrongdoings are sought to be investigated. CBI has powers but it is not independent. CVC is independent but it does not have sufficient powers or resources. ❑

8

What is Jan Lokpal Bill

The Jan Lokpal Bill (Citizen's ombudsman Bill) is a draft anti-corruption bill drawn up by prominent civil society activists seeking the appointment of a Jan Lokpal, an independent body that would investigate corruption cases, complete the investigation within a year and envisages trial in the case getting over in the next one year.

Drafted by Justice Santosh Hegde (former Supreme Court Judge and present Lokayukta of Karnataka), Prashant Bhushan (Supreme Court Lawyer) and Arvind Kejriwal (RTI activist), the draft Bill envisages a system where a corrupt person found guilty would go to jail within two years of the complaint being made and his ill-gotten wealth being confiscated. It also seeks power to the Jan Lokpal to prosecute politicians and bureaucrats without government permission.

Retired IPS officer Kiran Bedi and other known people like Swami Agnivesh, Sri Sri Ravi Shankar, Anna Hazare and Mallika Sarabhai are also part of the movement, called India Against Corruption. Its website describes the movement as "an expression of collective anger of people of India against corruption. We have all come together to force/request/persuade/pressurize the Government to enact the Jan Lokpal Bill. We feel that if this Bill were enacted it would create an effective deterrence against corruption."

10 Main Features of Jan Lokpal Bill

1. An institution called **Lokpal** at the centre and **Lokayukta** in each state will be set up.
2. Like Supreme Court and Election Commission, they will be completely independent of the governments. No minister or bureaucrat will be able to influence their investigations.
3. Cases against corrupt people will not linger on for years anymore. Investigations in any case will have to be completed in one year. Trial should be completed in next one year so that the corrupt politician, officer or judge is sent to jail within two years.
4. The loss that a corrupt person caused to the government will be recovered at the time of conviction.
5. How will it help a common citizen– If any work of any citizen is not done in prescribed time in any government office, Lokpal will impose financial penalty on guilty officers, which will be given as compensation to the complainant.
6. So, you could approach Lokpal if your ration card or passport or voter card is not being made or if police is not registering your case or any other work is not being done in prescribed time. Lokpal will have to get it done in a month's time. You could also report any case of

corruption to Lokpal like ration being siphoned off, poor quality roads been constructed or panchayat funds being siphoned off. Lokpal will have to complete its investigations in a year, trial will be over in next one year and the guilty will go to jail within two years.

7. But won't the government appoint corrupt and weak people as Lokpal members? That won't be possible because its members will be selected by judges, citizens and constitutional authorities and not by politicians, through a completely transparent and participatory process.
8. What if some officer in Lokpal becomes corrupt? The entire functioning of Lokpal/Lokayukta will be completely transparent. Any complaint against any officer of Lokpal shall be investigated and the officer will be dismissed within two months.
9. What will happen to existing anti-corruption agencies? CVC, departmental vigilance and anti-corruption branch of CBI will be merged into Lokpal. Lokpal will have complete powers and machinery to independently investigate and prosecute any officer, judge or politician.
10. It will be the duty of the Lokpal to provide protection to those who are being victimized for raising their voice against corruption.

❑

9

Draft of Jan Lokpal Bill

An act to create effective anti-corruption and grievance redressal systems at centre so that effective deterrent is created against corruption and to provide effective protection to whistleblowers.

1. Short title and commencement

(1) This Act may be called the Anti-Corruption, Grievance Redressal And Whistleblower Protection Act, 2010.

(2) It shall come into force on the one hundred and twentieth day of its enactment.

2. Definitions

In this Act, unless the context otherwise requires—

(1) "Action" means any action taken by a public servant in the discharge of his functions as such public servant and includes decision, recommendation or finding or in any other manner and includes willful failure or omission to act and all other expressions relating to such action shall be construed accordingly.

(2) "Allegation" in relation to a public servant includes any affirmation that such public servant- (a) has indulged in misconduct, if he is a government servant; (b) has indulged in corruption.

(3) "Complaint" includes any grievance or allegation or a request by whistleblower for protection and appropriate action.

(4) "Corruption" includes anything made punishable under Chapter IX of the Indian Penal Code or under the Prevention of Corruption Act, 1988.

(5) "Government" or "Central Government" means Government of India.

(6) "Government Servant" means any person who is or was any time appointed to a civil service or post in connection with the affairs of the Central Government or High Courts or Supreme Court either on deputation or permanent or temporary or on contractual employment but would not include the judges.

(7) "Grievance" means a claim by a person that he sustained injustice or undue hardship in consequence of mal-administration.

(8) "Lokpal" means: (a) Benches constituted under this Act and performing their functions as laid down under various provisions of this Act; or (b) Any officer or employee, exercising its powers and carrying out its functions and responsibilities, in the manner and to the extent, assigned to it under this Act, or under various rules, regulations or orders made under various provisions of this Act. (c) For all other purposes, the Chairperson and members acting collectively as a body.

(9) "Mal-administration" means action taken or purporting to have been taken in the exercise of administrative function in any case where—(a) such action or the administrative procedure or practice governing such action is unreasonable, unjust, oppressive or improperly discriminatory; or (b) there has been willful negligence or undue delay in taking

such action or the administrative procedure or practice governing such action involves undue delay.

(10) "Misconduct" means misconduct as defined in CCS Conduct Rules and which has vigilance angle.

(11) "Public authority" means any authority or body or institution of self- government established or constituted— (a) by or under the Constitution; (b) by any other law made by Parliament; (c) by notification issued or order made by the Government, and includes anybody owned, controlled or substantially financed by the Government.

(12) "Public servant" means a person who is or was at any time—(a) the Prime Minister; (b) a Minister; (c) a Member of Parliament; (d) Judges of High Courts and Supreme Court; (e) a Government servant; (f) the Chairman or Vice-Chairman (by whatever name called) or a member of a local authority in the control of the Central Government or a statutory body or corporation established by or under any law of the Parliament of India, including a co-operative society, or a Government Company within the meaning of section 617 of the Companies Act, 1956 and members of any Committee or Board, statutory or non-statutory, constituted by the Government; (g) Such other authorities as the Central Government may, by notification, from time to time, specify.

(13) "Vigilance angle" includes - (a) All acts of corruption (b)Gross or willful negligence; recklessness in decision making; blatant violations of systems and procedures; exercise of discretion in excess, where no ostensible/public interest is evident; failure to keep the controlling authority/superiors informed in time (c) Failure/delay in taking action, if under law the government servant ought to do so, against subordinates on complaints of corruption or dereliction of duties or abuse of office by the

subordinates (d) Indulging in discrimination through one's conduct, directly or indirectly (e) Victimizing Whistle Blowers (f) Any undue/unjustified delay in the disposal of a case, perceived after considering all relevant factors, would reinforce a conclusion as to the presence of vigilance angle in a case. (g) Make or undertake an unfair investigation or enquiry either to unduly help those guilty of corruption or incriminate the innocent. (h) Any other matter as notified from time to time by Lokpal.

(14) Make unfair investigation or enquiry to either unduly help culprits or fabricate the innocent.

(15) "Whistleblower" is any person who faces threat of (1) professional harm, including but not limited to illegitimate transfers, denial of promotions, denial of appropriate perks, departmental proceedings, discrimination or (2) physical harm or (3) is actually subjected to such harm; because of either making a complaint to Lokpal under this Act or for filing an application under Right to Information Act.

3. Establishment of the institution of Lokpal and appointment of Lokpal:

(1) There shall be an institution known as Lokpal which shall consist of one Chairperson and ten members along with its officers and employees. The Lokpal shall be headed by its Chairperson.

(2) The Chairperson and members of Lokpal shall be selected in such manner as laid down in this Act.

(3) A person appointed as Chairperson or member of Lokpal shall, before entering upon his office, make and subscribe before the President, an oath or affirmation in the form as prescribed.

(4) The Government shall appoint the Chairperson and members of the first Lokpal and set up the institution with all its logistics and assets within six months of enactment of this Act.

(5) The Government shall fill up a vacancy of the Chairperson or a member caused due to (a) Retirement, 3 months before the member or the Chairperson retires. (b) Any other unforeseen reason, within a month of such vacancy.

Chairperson and Members of Lokpal

4. The Chairperson and members of Lokpal not to have held certain offices-

The Chairperson and members of Lokpal shall not be serving or former member of either the Parliament or the Legislature of any State and shall not hold any office or trust of profit (other than the office as Chairperson or member) or would have ever been connected with any political party or carry on any business or practice any profession and accordingly, before he enters upon his office, a person appointed as the Chairperson or member of Lokpal shall-

(i) If he holds any office of trust or profit, resign from such office; or

(ii) if he is carrying on any business, sever his connection with the conduct and management of such business; or

(iii) if he is practicing any profession, suspend practice of such profession.

(iv) If he is associated directly or indirectly with any other activity, which is likely cause conflict of interest in the performance of his duties in Lokpal, he should suspend his association with that activity.

Provided that if even after the suspension, the earlier association of that person with such activity is likely to adversely affect his performance at Lokpal, that person shall not be appointed as a member or Chairperson of Lokpal.

5. Term of office and other conditions of service of Lokpal–

(1) A person appointed as the Chairperson or member of Lokpal shall hold office for a term of five years from the date on which he enters upon his office;

Provided further that-

(a) The Chairperson or member of Lokpal may, by writing under his hand addressed to the President, resign his office.

(b) The Chairperson or member may be removed from office in the manner provided in this Act.

(2) There shall be paid to the Chairperson and each member every month a salary equal to that of the Chief Justice of India and that of the judge of the Supreme Court respectively.

(3) The allowances and pension payable to and other conditions of service of the Chairperson or a member shall be such as may be prescribed, provided that the allowances and pension payable to and other conditions of service of the Chairperson or members shall not be varied to his disadvantage after his appointment.

(4) The administrative expenses of the office of the Lokpal including all salaries, allowances and pensions payable to or in respect of persons serving in that office, shall be charged on the Consolidated Fund of India.

(5) There shall be a separate fund by the name of "Lokpal fund" in which penalties/fines imposed by the Lokpal shall be deposited and in which 10% of the loss of Public Money detected/prevented on account of investigations by Lokpal shall also be deposited by the Government. Disposal of such fund shall be completely at the discretion of the Lokpal and such fund shall be used only for enhancement/upgradation/extension of the infrastructure of Lokpal.

(6) The Chairperson or members shall not be eligible for appointment on any position in Government of India or Government of any state or for fighting elections, if he has ever held the position of the Chairperson or a member for any period.

Provided however that a member or Chairperson may be reappointed for one more term or a member may be appointed as the Chairperson, however, that any person shall not serve for more than a total of two terms.

6. Appointment of the Chairperson and members:

1. The Chairperson and members shall be appointed by the President on the recommendation of a selection committee.

2. Following persons shall not be eligible to become Chairman or Member in Lokpal:

(a) Any person who was ever chargesheeted for any offence under IPC or PC Act or was ever penalized under CCS Conduct Rules.

(b) Any person who is less than 40 years in age.

3. At least four members of Lokpal shall have legal background.

4. A selection committee consisting of the following shall be set up:

(a) Two senior most judges of Supreme Court

(b) Two senior most Chief Justices of High Courts

(c) All Nobel Laureates of Indian Origin

(d) Last three Magsaysay Award winners

(e) Comptroller and Auditor General of India

(f) Chief Election Commissioner

(g) After the first set of selection process, the outgoing members and Chairperson of Lokpal

5. The senior-most judge of Supreme Court shall act as the Chairperson of the selection committee.

6. The following selection process shall be followed:

(a) Recommendations shall be invited through open advertisements in prescribed format.

(b) The candidates should have unimpeachable integrity and should have demonstrated their resolve and efforts to fight against corruption in the past.

(c) Each person recommending shall be expected to justify the selection of his candidate giving examples from the past achievements of the candidate.

(d) The list of candidates along with their recommendations received in the format mentioned above shall be displayed on a website.

(e) Each member of the selection committee, on the basis of the above material, shall recommend such number of names as there are vacancies.

(f) A priority list shall be prepared with the candidate receiving recommendations from maximum number of members of selection committee at the top. The candidates recommended by same number of members shall be treated at par.

(g) This priority list shall be displayed on the website.

(h) Around three times the names as there are vacancies, shall be shortlisted from the top.

(i) Public feedback shall be invited on the shortlisted names by putting these names on the website.

(j) The selection committee may decide to use any means to collect more information about the background and past achievements of the shortlisted candidates.

(k) Selection committee shall invite shortlisted candidates for discussions, video recordings of which shall be made public.

(l) All the material obtained so far about the candidates shall be made available to each member of the selection committee in advance. The members shall make their own assessment of each candidate.

(m) The selection committee shall meet and discuss the material so received about each candidate. The final selections for the Chairperson and members shall be made preferably through consensus.

Provided that if three or more members, for reasons to be recorded in writing, object to the selection of any member, he shall not be selected.

(n) All meetings of selection committee shall be video recorded and shall be made public.

7. Selection committee shall recommend the names to the President, who shall order such appointments within a month of receipt of the same.

7. Removal of Chairperson or members-

(1) The Chairperson or any member shall not be removed from his office except by an order of the President.

(2) They can be removed on one or more of the following grounds:

(a) Proved misbehavior

(b) Professional or physical incapacity

(c) If he is adjudged to be insolvent

(d) Has been charged of an offence which involves moral turpitude

(e) If he engages during his term of office in any paid employment outside the duties of his office

(f) Has acquired such financial interests or other interests which are likely to affect prejudicially his functions as member or Chairperson.

(g) If he is guided by considerations extraneous to the merits of the case either to favour someone or to implicate someone through any act of omission or commission.

(h) If he commits any act of omission or commission which is punishable under Prevention of Corruption Act or is a misconduct.

(i) If a member or the Chairperson in any way, concerned or interested in any contract or agreement made by or on behalf of the Government of India or participates in any way in the profit thereof or in any benefit or emolument arising there from otherwise than as a member and in common with the other members of an incorporated company, he shall be deemed to be guilty of misbehavior.

(3) The following process shall be followed for the removal of any member or Chairperson:

(a) Any person may move an application/petition before the Supreme Court seeking removal of one or more of the members of Chairperson of Lokpal alleging one or more of the grounds for removal and providing evidence for the same.

(b) Supreme Court will hear the matter by a bench of three or more Judges on receipt of such petition and may take one or more of the following steps:

(i) Order an investigation to be done by a Special Investigation Team appointed by the Supreme Court if a prima facie case is made out and if the matter cannot be judged based on affidavits of the parties.

(ii) Dismiss the petition if no case is made out.

(iii) If the grounds are proved, recommend to the President for removal of the said member or Chairperson.

(iv) Direct registration and investigation of cases with appropriate agencies if there is prima facie case of commission of an offence punishable under Prevention of Corruption Act.

(c) The Supreme Court shall not dismiss such petitions in liminae.

(d) If the Supreme Court concludes that the petition has been made with mischievous or malafide motives, the Court may order imposition of fine or imprisonment upto one year against the complainant.

(e) On receipt of a recommendation from the Supreme Court under this section, the President shall order removal of said members within a month of receipt of the same.

Powers and Functions of Lokpal

8. Functions of Lokpal:

(1) Lokpal shall be responsible for receiving:

(a) Complaints where there are allegations of such acts of omission or commission which are punishable under Prevention of Corruption Act

(b) Complaints where there are allegations of misconduct by a government servant

(c) Grievances

(d) Complaints from whistleblowers

(2) Lokpal, after getting such enquiries and investigations done as it deems fit, may take one or more of the following actions:

(a) Close the case if prima facie, the complaint is not made out or

(b) Initiate prosecution against public servants as well as those private entities which are party to the act

(c) Order imposition of appropriate penalties under CCS Conduct Rules

Provided that if an officer is finally convicted under Prevention of Corruption Act, major penalty of dismissal shall be imposed on such government servant.

(d) Order cancellation or modification of a license or lease or permission or contract or agreement, which was the subject matter of investigation.

(e) Blacklist the concerned firm or company or contractor or any other entity involved in that act of corruption.

(f) Issue appropriate directions to appropriate authorities for redressal of grievance in such time and in such manner as is specified in the order.

(g) Invoke its powers under this Act if its orders are not duly complied with and ensure due compliance of its orders.

(h) Take necessary action to provide protection to a whistleblower as per various provisions of this Act.

(3) Suo moto initiate appropriate action under this Act if any case, of the nature mentioned in clauses (1), (2), (3) or (4), comes to the knowledge of the Lokpal from any source.

(4) Issue such directions, as are necessary, from time to time, to appropriate authorities so as to make such changes in their work practices, administration or other systems so as to reduce the scope and possibility for corruption, misconduct and public grievances.

(5) Lokpal shall be deemed to be "Disciplinary authority" or "appointing authority" for the purpose of imposing penalties under CCS Conduct Rules.

(6) Section 19 of Prevention of Corruption Act shall be deleted.

(7) Section 197 of CrPC shall not apply to any proceedings under this Act. All permissions, which need to be sought for initiating investigations or for initiating prosecutions under any Act shall be deemed to have been granted once Lokpal grants such permissions.

9. Issue of Search Warrant, etc.

(1) Where, in consequence of information in his possession, the Lokpal

(a) has reason to believe that any person–

(i) to whom a summon or notice under this Act, has, been or might be issued, will not or would not produce or cause to be produced any property, document or thing which will be necessary or useful for or relevant to any inquiry or other proceeding to be conducted by him;

(ii) is in possession of any money, bullion, jewellery or other valuable article or thing and such money, bullion, jewellery or other valuable article or thing represents either wholly or partly income or property which has not been disclosed to the authorities for the purpose of any law or rule in force which requires such disclosure to be made; or

(b) considers that the purposes of any inquiry or other proceedings to be conducted by him will be served by a general search or inspection, he may by a search warrant authorize any Police officer not below the rank of an Inspector of Police to conduct a search or carry out an inspection in accordance therewith and in particular to;

(i) enter and search any building or place where he has reason to suspect that such property, document, money, bullion, jewellery or other valuable article or thing is kept;

(ii) search any person who is reasonably suspected of concealing about his person any article for which search should be made;

(iii) break open the lock of any door, box, locker safe, almirah or other receptacle for exercising the powers conferred by sub-clause (i) where the keys thereof are not available.

Seize any such property, document, money, bullion, jewellery or other valuable article or thing found as a result of such search;

(iv) place marks of identification on any property or document or make or cause to be made; extracts or copies therefrom; or

(v) make a note or an inventory of any such property, document, money, bullion, Jewellery or other valuable article or thing.

(2) The provisions of the Code of Criminal Procedure, 1973, relating to search and seizure shall apply, so far as may be, to searches and seizures under sub-section (1).

(3) A warrant issued under sub-section (1) shall for all purposes, be deemed to be a warrant issued by a court under section 93 of the Code of Criminal Procedure, 1973.

10. Evidence

(1) Subject to the provisions of this section, for the purpose of any investigation (including the preliminary inquiry, if any, before such investigation) under this Act, the Lokpal may require any public servant or any other person who, in his opinion is able to furnish information or produce documents relevant to the investigation, to furnish any such information or produce any such document.

(2) For the purpose of any such investigation (including the preliminary inquiry) the Lokpal shall have all the powers of a civil court while trying a suit under the Code of Civil Procedure, 1908, in respect of the following matters, namely-

(a) Summoning and enforcing the attendance of any person and examining him on oath;

(b) Requiring the discovery and production of any document;

(c) Receiving evidence on affidavits;

(d) Requisitioning any public record or copy thereof from any court or office;

(e) Issuing commissions for the examination of witnesses or documents;

(f) Ordering payment of compensatory cost in respect of a false or vexatious claim or defence;

(g) Ordering cost for causing delay;

(h) Such other matters as may be prescribed.

(3) Any proceeding before the Lokpal shall be deemed to be a judicial proceeding within the meaning of section 193 of the Indian Penal Code.

11. Reports of Lokpal, etc.

(1) The Chairperson of Lokpal shall present annually a consolidated report in prescribed format on its performance to the President.

(2) On receipt of the annual report, the President shall cause a copy thereof together with an explanatory memorandum to be laid before each House of the Parliament.

(3) The Lokpal shall publish every month on its website the list of cases disposed with brief details of each such case, outcome and action taken or proposed to be taken in that case. It shall also publish lists of all cases received by the Lokpal during the previous month, cases disposed and cases which are pending.

12. Lokpal to be a deemed police officer:

(1) For the purposes of section 36 of Criminal Procedure Code, the Chairperson, members of Lokpal and the officers in investigation wing of Lokpal shall be deemed to be police officers.

(2) While investigating any offence under Prevention of Corruption Act 1988, they shall be competent to investigate any offence under any other law in the same case.

13. Powers in case of non-compliance of orders:

(1) Each order of Lokpal shall clearly specify the names of the officials who are required to execute that order,

the manner in which it should be executed and the time period within which that order should be complied with.

(2) If the order is not complied with within the time or in the manner directed, Lokpal may decide to impose a fine on the officials responsible for the non-compliance of its orders.

(3) The Drawing and Disbursing Officer of that Department shall be directed to deduct such amount of fine as is clearly specified by the Lokpal in its order made in sub-section (2) from the salaries of the officers specified in the order.

Provided that no penalty shall be imposed without giving a reasonable opportunity of being heard.

Provided that if the Drawing and Disbursing Officer fails to deduct the salary as specified in the said order, he shall make himself liable for a similar penalty.

(3) In order to get its orders complied with, the Lokpal shall have, and exercise the same jurisdiction powers and authority in respect of contempt of itself as a High court has and may exercise, and for this purpose, the provisions of the Contempt of Courts Act, 1971 (Central Act 70 of 1971) shall have the effect subject to the modification that the references therein to the High Court shall be construed as including a reference to the Lokpal.

13A. Special Judges under section 4 of Prevention of Corruption Act:

On an annual basis, Lokpal shall make an assessment of the number of Special Judges required under section 4 of Prevention of Corruption Act 1988 in each area and the Government shall appoint such number of Judges within three months of receipt of such recommendation.

Provided that Lokpal shall recommend such number of Special Judges so that trial in each case under this Act is completed within a year.

Functioning of Lokpal

14. Functioning of Lokpal:

(1) The Chairperson shall be responsible for overall administration and supervision of the institution of Lokpal.

(2) All policy level decisions including formulation of regulations, developing internal systems for the functioning of Lokpal, assigning functions to various officials in Lokpal, delegation of powers to various functionaries in Lokpal etc shall be taken by the Chairperson and the members collectively as a body.

(3) The Chairperson shall have an annual meeting with the Prime Minister to assess the needs of Lokpal for finances and manpower. Lokpal shall be provided resources by the Government on the basis of outcome of this meeting.

(4) Lokpal shall function in benches of three or more members. Benches shall be constituted randomly and cases shall be assigned to them randomly by computer. Each bench shall consist of at least one member with legal background.

(5) Such benches shall be responsible for

(i) granting permission to close any case after a preliminary enquiry

(ii) granting permission to either close a case after investigations or issuing orders imposing penalties under CCS Conduct Rules and/or for initiating prosecution in that case.

(iii) Issuing orders under section 28.

(6) Lokpal may decide to initiate investigations into any case suo moto also.

(7) Chairperson shall chair all meetings of Lokpal.

(8) The decision to initiate investigation or prosecution against any member of the Cabinet or any judge of High Court or Supreme Court shall be taken in a meeting of all the existing members and the Chairperson. Minutes and records of such meetings shall be made public.

15. Making a complaint to the Lokpal:

(1) Subject to the provisions of this Act, any person may make a complaint under this Act to the Lokpal.

Provided that in case of a grievance, if the person aggrieved is dead or for any reason, unable to act for himself, the complaint may be made or if it is already made may be continued by his legal representatives or by any other person who is authorized by him in writing in this behalf.

(2) A complaint could be on a plain paper but should contain all such details as prescribed by Lokpal.

(3) On receipt of a complaint, the Lokpal shall decide whether it is an allegation or a grievance or a request for whistleblower protection or a mixture of two or more of these.

(4) Every complaint shall have to be compulsorily disposed off by the Lokpal.

Provided that no complaint, other than those which are anonymous, shall be closed without hearing the complainant.

16. Matters which may be investigated by the Lokpal–

Subject to the provisions of this Act, the Lokpal may investigate any action which is taken by or with the general or specific approval of a public servant where a complaint involving a grievance or an allegation is made in respect of such action.

Provided that the Lokpal may also investigate such action suo moto or if it is referred to it by the government, if such action can be or could have been in his recorded opinion, subject of a grievance or an allegation.

17. Matters not subject to investigation-

(1) The Lokpal shall not conduct any investigation under thisAct in case of a grievance in respect of any action.

(i) if the complainant has or had, any remedy by way of appeal, revision, review or any other remedy before any other authority provided in any other law and he has not availed of the same.

(ii) Taken by a judicial or quasi-judicial body, unless the complainant alleges malafides

(iii) If the substance of the entire grievance is pending before any court or quasi-judicial body of competent jurisdiction.

(iv) Any grievance where there is inordinate and inexplicable delay.

(2) Nothing in this Act shall be construed as authorising the Lokpal to investigate any action which is taken by or with the approval of the Presiding Officer of either House of Parliament.

(3) The provisions of this Act shall be in addition to the provisions of any other enactment or any rule or law under which any remedy by way of appeal, revision, review or in any other manner is available to a person making a complaint under this Act in respect of any action and nothing in this Act shall limit or affect the right of such person to avail of such remedy.

(4) Nothing in this section shall bar Lokpal from entertaining a complaint making an allegation of misconduct or corruption or a complaint from a whistleblower seeking protection.

18. Provisions relating to complaints and investigations-

(i) (a) The Lokpal, on receipt of a complaint in the nature of an allegation or a grievance or a combination of the two, or in a case initiated on his own motion, may on perusing the documents, either decide to proceed to enquire or investigate into that complaint or decide, to make such preliminary inquiry before proceeding to enquire or investigate into such complaint or direct any other person to make such preliminary inquiry as it deems fit for ascertaining whether there exists reasonable ground for conducting the investigation. The outcome of such preliminary enquiry, and if the complaint is being closed along with reasons for the same and all material collected during preliminary enquiry, shall be communicated to the complainant.

Provided that if any case is closed, all documents related thereto shall thereafter be treated as public. Every month, a list of all such cases shall be put on the website with reasons for closing a case. All material connected with such closed cases will be provided to anyone seeking it under Right to Information Act.

Provided further that if the complaint contains verifiable and specific information about misconduct or corruption, then that case shall not be rejected even if the complaint is anonymous.

Provided further that no complaint of allegation shall be rejected by questioning the motives or intention of the complainant.

Provided further that all hearings before Lokpal shall be video recorded and shall be available to any member of the public on payment of copying costs.

(b) The procedure for preliminary enquiry of a complaint shall be such as the Lokpal deems appropriate in the circumstances of the case and in particular, the Lokpal may, if it deems necessary to do so, call for the comments of the public servant concerned.

Provided that the preliminary enquiry should be completed and a decision taken whether to close a case or to proceed with investigations within one month of receipt of any complaint.

(ii) Where the Lokpal proposes, either directly or after making preliminary inquiry, to conduct any investigation under this Act, he-

(a) may make such order as to the safe custody of documents relevant to the investigation, as it deems fit.

(b) at appropriate stage of investigations or in the end, it shall forward a copy of the complaint, its findings and copy of the material relied upon to the concerned public servant and the complainant,

(c) shall afford to such public servant and the complainant an opportunity to offer comments and be heard.

Provided that such hearing shall be held in public, except in such rare circumstances, to be recorded in writing, will it be held in camera.

(iii) The conduct of an investigation under this Act against a Public servant in respect of any action shall not affect such action, or any power or duty of any other public servant to take further action with respect to any matter subject to the investigation.

(iv)If, during the course of preliminary inquiry or investigation under this Act, the Lokpal is prima facie satisfied that the allegation or grievance in respect of any action is likely to be sustained either wholly or partly, he may, through an interim order, direct the public servant concerned to stay the implementation or enforcement of the decision or action complained against, or to take such mandatory or preventive action, on such terms and conditions, as he may specify in his order to prevent further harm from taking place.

(v) The Lokpal, either during the course of investigations, if it is satisfied that prosecution is likely to be initiated in that case, or at the end of the investigations at the time of initiating prosecution, shall make a list of the assets of all the accused in that case and shall notify the same. In the event of final conviction, the court shall be empowered to recover loss determined under section 19 of this Act from this property and any transfer of property subsequent to the date of notification by Lokpal under this sub-section shall be treated as null and void.

(vi) If during the course of investigation or enquiry into a complaint, Lokpal feels that continuance of a public servant in that position could adversely affect the course of investigations or enquiry or that the said person is likely to impact evidence or witnesses, the Lokpal may issue appropriate orders including transfer of that public servant from that position or his suspension.

Provided that such orders shall not be passed against the Prime Minister.

(vii) In case of a grievance, the Lokpal may issue interim orders to the appropriate authority recommending grant of interim relief to the complainant if he is satisfied at any stage of preliminary inquiry on investigation that the complainant has sustained injustice or undue hardship in consequence of any decision or action of a public servant.

(viii)The Lokpal may, at any stage of inquiry or investigation under this Act, direct through an interim order, appropriate authorities to take such action as is necessary, including suspension of a government servant, pending inquiry or investigation.-

i. to safeguard wastage or damage of public property or public revenue by the administrative acts of the public servant;

ii. to prevent further acts of misconduct by the public servant;

iii. to prevent the public servant from secreting the assets allegedly acquired by him by corrupt means;

(ix) Where after investigation into a complaint, the Lokpal is satisfied that the complaint involving an allegation against the public servant is substantiated and that the public servant concerned should not continue to hold the post held by him, the Lokpal shall pass orders to that effect. If that public servant is a government servant, he shall be deemed to have vacated the position with effect from receipt of such order. In case of public servants other than government servants, Lokpal shall make such recommendation to the President, who shall decide either to accept such recommendation or reject it within a month of its receipt.

(x) If, after enquiry into a grievance and after affording reasonable opportunity of being heard to both the complainant and the public authority, the Lokpal is satisfied that such grievance is substantiated either wholly or partly, he shall,

i. Pass appropriate orders directing appropriate authorities to redress the grievance in a manner and within the time prescribed in the order, and

ii. Direct the appropriate authorities to deduct from the salary of the officials mentioned in the order amounts calculated and specified in the order at the rate of Rs 250 per day of delay calculated from day the time limit mentioned in citizens' charter for redressing that grievance got over, and

iii. Direct the appropriate authorities to compensate the complainant with such amounts as mentioned in the order.

Provided that any grievance shall be disposed within 15 days of its receipt.

Provided further that if it relates to life and liberty of a person or if the matter is such as to warrant immediate attention and the Lokpal is so satisfied, the same shall be disposed within 48 hours.

(xi) All records and information of Lokpal shall be public and shall be provided under Right to Information Act, even at the stage of investigation or enquiry, unless release of such information would adversely affect the process of enquiry or investigation.

Provided that no information in any case shall be withheld under Right to Information Act after the completion of enquiry or investigation.

Recovery of Loss to the Government and Punishments

19. Recovery of loss to the Government:

If a person is convicted of an offence under Prevention of Corruption Act, then the trial court will also quantify the loss caused to the government and apportion that amount to various convicts from whom this money must be recovered as arrears of land revenue.

19A. Punishments for offences:

For offences mentioned in Chapter III of Prevention of Corruption Act, punishment shall not be less than five years which may extend up to life imprisonment.

Whistleblower Protection

20. Protection of Whistleblower:

(1) A whistleblower may write to Lokpal seeking protection from threat of physical or professional victimization or if he has been subjected to such professional or physical victimization.

fast track and complete investigations in that case in such time as directed by the Lokpal.

(2) Lokpal shall have the powers to issue directions to appropriate agencies in the cases covered under clause (f), monitor such investigations and if necessary, issue directions to that agency to do the investigations in the manner as directed by the Lokpal.

(3) If any complainant requests that his identity should be kept secret, Lokpal shall ensure the same. Lokpal shall prescribe detailed procedures on how such complainants shall be dealt with.

(4) Lokpal shall Issue orders to the Public Authorities to make necessary changes in their policies and practices to prevent recurrence of victimization.

Grievance Redressal Systems

21. Citizens' Charters:

(1) Each public authority shall be responsible for ensuring the preparation and implementation of Citizens

Charter, within a reasonable time, and not exceeding one year from the coming into force of this Act.

(2) Every Citizens Charter shall enumerate the commitments of the respective public authority to the citizens, officer responsible for meeting each such commitment and the time limit with in which the commitment shall be met.

(3) Each public authority shall designate an official called Public Grievance Redressal Officer, whom a complainant should approach for any violation of the Citizens Charter.

(4) Every public authority shall review and revise its Citizens Charter at least once every year through a process of public consultation.

(5) Lokpal may direct any public authority to make such changes in their citizens' charter as are mentioned in that order.

(6) No grievance shall be accepted by Lokpal if 15 days have not elapsed after submission of complaint by the complainant with the Public Grievance redressal Officer of that Public Authority.

Provided that if Lokpal feels that considering the gravity or urgency of the grievance, it is necessary to do so, the Lokpal may decide to accept such grievance earlier also.

Employees and staff and authorities in Lokpal

22. Chief Vigilance Officer:

(1) There shall be a Chief Vigilance Officer in each public authority to be selected and appointed by Lokpal.

(2) He shall not be from the same public authority.

(3) He shall be a person of impeccable integrity and ability to take proactive measures against corruption.

(4) He shall be responsible for accepting complaints against any public authority and shall transfer the complaints related to other public authorities within two days of receipt.

(5) He shall be responsible for carrying out all such responsibilities as assigned to him from time to time by Lokpal including dealing with complaints in the manner as laid down by Lokpal from time to time.

Provided that the complaints which require investigations under Prevention of Corruption Act 1988 shall be transferred to the Investigative wing of Lokpal.

Provided further that the complaints, other than grievances, against officers of the level of Joint Secretary or above shall not be dealt by the Chief Vigilance Officer and shall be transferred to the Lokpal, who shall set up a committee of Chief Vigilance Officers of three other public authorities to enquire into such complaint.

23. Staff of Lokpal, etc.-

(1) There shall be such officers and employees as may be prescribed to assist the Lokpal in the discharge of their functions under this Act.

(2) The number and categories of officers and employees shall be decided by the Lokpal in consultation with the government.

(3) The categories, recruitment and conditions of service of the officers and employees referred in sub-section (1) including such special conditions or special pay as may be necessary for enabling them to act without fear

in the discharge of their functions, shall be such as may be prescribed according to the recommendations of Lokpal.

Provided that no official, whose integrity is in doubt, shall be considered for being posted in Lokpal.

Provided further that all officers and employees, who work in Lokpal on deputation or otherwise shall be eligible for the same terms and conditions as prescribed under this clause.

(4) Without prejudice to the provisions of sub-section (1), the Lokpal may for the purpose of conducting investigations under this Act utilize the services of-

(a) any officer or investigating agency of the Government; or

(b) any officer or investigating agency of the Government with the prior concurrence of that Government; or

(c) any person or any other agency.

(5) The officers and other employees referred to in sub-section (1) shall be under the administrative and disciplinary control of the Lokpal:

(6) Lokpal shall have the powers to choose its own officials. Lokpal may enlist officials on deputation from other government agencies for a fixed tenure or it may enlist officials on permanent basis from other government agencies or it may appoint people from outside on permanent basis or on a fixed tenure basis.

(7) The staff and officers shall be entitled to such pay scales and other allowances, which may be different and more than the ordinary pay scales in the Central Government, as are decided by the Lokpal from time to time, in consultation with the Prime Minister, so as to attract honest and efficient people to work in Lokpal.

24. Repeal and savings -

(1) The Central Vigilance Commission Act shall stand repealed.

(2) Notwithstanding such repeal, any act or thing done under the said Act shall be deemed to have been done under this Act and may be continued and completed under the corresponding provisions of this Act.

(3) All enquiries and investigations and other disciplinary proceedings pending before the Central Vigilance Commission and which have not been disposed of, shall stand transferred to and be continued by the Lokpal as if they were commenced before him under this Act.

(4) Notwithstanding anything contained in any Act, the posts of the Secretary and other Officers and Employees of the Central Vigilance Commission are hereby abolished and they are hereby appointed as the Secretary and other officers and employees of the Lokpal. The salaries, allowances and other terms and conditions of services of the said Secretary, officers and other employees shall, until they are varied, be the same as to which they were entitled to immediately before the commencement of this Act.

(5) All vigilance administration under the control of all Departments of Central Government, Ministries of the Central Government, corporations established by or under any Central Act, Government companies, societies and local authorities owned or controlled by the Central Government shall stand transferred, alongwith its personnel, assets and liabilities to Lokpal for all purposes.

(6) The personnel working in vigilance wings of the agencies mentioned in sub-section (5) shall be deemed

to be on deputation to Lokpal for a period of five years from the date they are transferred to Lokpal. However, Lokpal may decide to repatriate any one of them anytime.

(7) That Department from where any personnel have been transferred to Lokpal under sub-section (5), shall cease to have any control over the administration and functions of transferred personnel.

(8) Lokpal shall rotate the personnel and create vigilance wing of each department in such a way that no personnel from the same department get posted for vigilance functions in the same department.

(9) No person shall be employed with Lokpal against whom any vigilance enquiry or any criminal case is pending at the time of being considered.

25. Investigation Wing of Lokpal:

(1) There shall be an investigation wing at Lokpal.

(2) Notwithstanding anything contained in section 17 of Prevention of Corruption Act, such officers of

Investigation wing, upto the level as decided by Lokpal, shall have, in relation to the investigation and arrest of persons throughout India, in connection with investigation of complaints under this Act, all the powers, duties, privileges and liabilities which members of Delhi Special Police Establishment have in connection with the investigation of offences committed therein.

(3) That part of Delhi Special Police Establishment, in so far as it relates to investigation and prosecution of offences alleged to have been committed under the Prevention of Corruption Act, 1988, shall stand

transferred, alongwith its employees, assets and liabilities to Lokpal for all purposes.

(4) That part of Delhi Special Police Establishment, which has been transferred under sub-section (3), shall form part of Investigation Wing of Lokpal.

(5) The Central Government shall cease to have any control over the transferred part and its personnel.

(6) The salaries, allowances and other terms and conditions of services of the personnel transferred under sub-section (3) shall be the same as to which they were entitled to immediately before the commencement of this Act.

(7) All cases which were being dealt by that part of Delhi Special Police Establishment, which has been transferred under sub-section (3), shall stand transferred to Lokpal.

(8) After completion of investigation in any case, the investigation wing shall present the case to an appropriate bench of Lokpal, which shall decide whether to grant permission for prosecution or not.

26. Complaints against officers or employees of Lokpal:

(1) Complaints against employees or officers of Lokpal shall be dealt with separately and as per provisions of this section.

(2) Such complaint could relate to an allegation of an offence punishable under Prevention of Corruption Act or a misconduct or a dishonest enquiry or investigation.

(3) As soon as such a complaint is received, the same shall be displayed on the website of Lokpal, along with the contents of the complaint.

(4) Investigations into each such complaint shall be completed within a month of its receipt.

(5) In addition to examining the allegations against the said official, the allegations shall especially be examined against sections 107, 166, 167, 177, 182, 191, 192, 196, 199, 200, 201, 202, 204, 217, 218, 219, 463, 464, 468, 469, 470, 471, 474 of Indian Penal Code.

(6) If, during the course of investigations, the Lokpal feels that the charges are likely to be sustained, the

Lokpal shall divest such officer of all his responsibilities and powers and shall place him under suspension.

(7) If after completion of enquiry or investigations, Lokpal decides to prosecute that person under Prevention of Corruption Act, 1988 or holds him guilty of any misconduct or of conducting dishonest enquiry or investigations, then that person shall not work with Lokpal anymore. Lokpal shall either dismiss that person from the job, if that person is in the employment of Lokpal, or shall repatriate him, if he is on deputation.

Provided that no order under this clause shall be passed without giving reasonable opportunity of being heard to the accused person.

Provided further that order under this clause shall be passed within 15 days of completion of investigations.

(8) There shall be a separate wing in Lokpal to deal with complaints against officers or staff of Lokpal.

(9) Lokpal shall take all steps to ensure that all enquiries and investigations on complaints against its own staff and officials are conducted in most transparent and honest manner.

27. Protection-

(1) No suit, prosecution, or other legal proceedings shall lie against the Chairperson or members or against any officer, employee, agency or person referred to in Section 14(4) in respect of anything which is in good faith done while acting or purporting to act in the discharge of his official duties under this Act.

(2) No proceedings of the Lokpal shall be held to be bad for want of form and except on the ground of jurisdiction, no proceedings or decision of the Lokpal shall be liable to be challenged, reviewed, quashed or called in question in any court of ordinary Civil Jurisdiction.

Miscellaneous

28. Public Servants to submit property statements-

(1) Every public servant, other than those mentioned in Section 2(11)(a) to (c), shall within three months after the commencement of this Act and thereafter before the 30th June of every year submit to the head of that public authority, in the form prescribed by Lokpal, a statement of his assets and liabilities and those of the members of his family. Public servants mentioned in sections 2(11)(a) to (c) shall submit their returns in a format prescribed by the Lokpal to the Lokpal with the aforesaid time lines.

(2) The Head of each public authority shall ensure that all such statements are put on the website by 31 August of that year.

(3) If no such statement is received by the Head of that public authority from any such public servant within the time specified in sub-section (1), the Head of that public authority shall direct the concerned public

servant to do so immediately. If within next one month, the public servant concerned does not submit such statement, the Head shall stop the salary and allowances of that public servant till he submits such statement.

Explanation- In this section "family of a public servant" means the spouse and such children and parents of the public servant as are dependent on him.

(4) The Lokpal may initiate prosecution against such public servant under Section 176 IPC.

(5) If any public servant furnishes any statement, which is subsequently found to be incorrect, then Lokpal, in addition to taking action against the said public servant under other sections of this Act, may also impose a penalty upto a maximum of 50% of the value of the additional property subsequently detected. Lokpal shall also intimate such information to the Income Tax Department for appropriate action.

29. Power to delegate and assign functions:

(1) Lokpal shall be competent to delegate its powers and assign functions to the officials working in Lokpal.

(2) All functions carried out and powers exercised by such officials shall be deemed to have been so done by the Lokpal.

Provided that the following functions shall be performed by the benches and cannot be delegated:

(i) Granting permission to initiate prosecution in any case.

(ii) Order for dismissal of any government servant under CCS Conduct Rules.

(iii) Passing orders under section 10 on complaints against officials and staff of Lokpal.

(iv) Pass orders in cases of complaints, other than grievances, against officers of the level of Joint Secretary and above.

30. Time limits:

(1) Preliminary enquiry under sub-section 1 of section 9 of this Act should be completed within a month of receipt of complaint.

Provided that the enquiry officer shall be liable for an explanation if the enquiry is not completed within this time limit.

(2) Investigation into any allegation shall be completed within six months, and in any case, not more than one year, from the date of receipt of complaint.

31. Penalty for false complaint-

(1) Notwithstanding anything contained in this Act, if someone makes any false or frivolous complaint under this Act, Lokpal may impose such fines on that complainant as it deems fit.

Provided that no fine can be imposed without giving a reasonable opportunity of being heard.

(2) Such fines shall be recoverable as dues under Land Revenue Act.

31A. Preventive measures:

(1) Lokpal shall, at regular intervals, either study itself or cause to be studied the functioning of all public authorities falling within its jurisdiction and in consultation with respective public authority, issue such directions as it deems fit to prevent incidence of corruption in future.

(2) Lokpal shall also be responsible for creating awareness about this Act and involving general public in curbing corruption and maladministration.

32. Power to make Rules -

(1) The Government may, by notification in the Official Gazette, make rules for the purpose of carrying into effect the provisions of this Act.

Provided that such rules shall be made only in consultation and with the approval of Lokpal.

(2) In particular, and without prejudice to the generality of the foregoing provisions, such rules may provide for -

(i) the allowance and pensions payable to and other conditions of service of the Chairperson and members of Lokpal;

(ii) the powers of a Civil Court which may be exercised by the Lokpal under clause (h) of sub-section 2 of section 11;

(iii) the salary, allowances, recruitment and other conditions of service of the staff and employees of the Lokpal;

(iv) any other matter for which rules have to be made are necessary under this Act.

(3) Any rule made under this Act may be made with retrospective effect and when such a rule is made the reasons for making the rule shall be specified in a Statement laid before both Houses of the Parliament.

33. Removal of difficulties-

Notwithstanding anything contained in this Act, the President, in consultation with Lokpal or on request of Lokpal may, by order, make such provision -

(i) for bringing the provisions of this Act into effective operation;

(ii) for continuing the enquiries and investigations pending before the Central Vigilance Commission by the Lokpal.

34. Power to make regulations:

Lokpal shall have power to make its own regulations for the smooth functioning of the institution and to effectively implement various provisions of this Act.

35. This Act shall override the provisions of all other laws.

Amendments in the Bill

The major changes later made in the bill are:

1. There is a higher 'political' involvement in process of choosing the Lokpal in the new version. It suggests, as members of the committee, the prime minister, the leader of opposition in the Lok Sabha, two youngest judges of the Supreme Court, two youngest chief justices of high courts, the Comptroller and Auditor General (CAG), and the Chief Election Commissioner (CEC).

   The earlier version had named the vice president, the Lok Sabha speaker, two senior-most judges of the Supreme Court, two senior-most chief justices of high courts, retired army personnel who are five-star generals, the chairperson of National Human Rights Commission, along with the CAG and the CEC.

   This was one of the most criticised clauses.

2. The selection process which was to be through an open advertisements in prescribed format, has been replaced by a search committee which will be composed of five

members, selected from former CAGs and CECs. The search committee will invite recommendations from such class of people or such individuals as it deems fit. It will recommend to the prime minister the names three times the number of vacancies that exist.

The earlier draft said recommendations shall be invited through open advertisements. The list of candidates along with their recommendations would then be displayed on the website and the shortlisting was to be done by the committee itself.

3. The earlier clause of minimum 10 years of punishment for officer of rank of joint secretary or above, and ministers has been dropped and the new version only says "punishment will be more severe if the accused is higher in rank".

The earlier version said: "Provided that if the accused is an officer of the rank of Joint Secretary or above or a Minister, a member or Chairperson of the Lokpal, the punishment shall not be less than ten years of imprisonment".

In addition to this, instead of two years of rigorous imprisonment extending up to life imprisonment, the minimum punishment is now one year.

4. For qualification for Lokpal, the clause for the person to be a citizen of India has been added to earlier existing clauses of being a person who was never charge-sheeted for any offence, never penalised and was less than 40 years old.

Major features of the Lokpal, as defined by the activists, however, remain same. The Lokpal will still get the complaints directly from people, will be empowered to take suo-motu actions and will have the powers of police.

❑

10

Major Differences between Government Bill & Jan Lokpal Bill

Citizen's Ombudsman Bill, popularly known as Jan Lokpal Bill is what the entire country demands from the government. Jan Lokpal Bill talks about a corruption free country. Jan Lokpal Bill is the anti-corruption bill which seeks the appointment of a Jan Lokpal. Jan Lokpal is demanded to be an independent basis, the idea for whose foundation is to investigate the corruption cases in the country.

The investigation of each of these cases would be complete within a year. The country is seeking an approval of the Jan Lokpal Bill drafted by Justice Santosh Hegde (Former Supreme Court Judge and Lokayukta of Karnataka), Prashant Bhushan (Supreme Court Lawyer) and Arvind Kejriwal (Right To Information activist). The Jan Lokpal Bill talks about a system where any person found guilty of corruption will get imprisonment within two year of the complaint. Moreover, his ill-gotten wealth will be confiscated. The bill empowers the Jan Lokpal to prosecute the bureaucrats and politicians without any permission from the government.

Well-known personalities like social activist Anna Hazare, retired IPS officer Kiran Bedi and dancer Mallika Sarabhai initiated the movement for Jan Lokpal Bill and the rest as they say is history. Jan Lokpal has become the voice of India. The kind of movement India has seen in the past few days shows how desperate are the Indians to make India a corruption-free nation!

Following are the major differences in the Existing System and System Proposed by Civil Society.

Existing System: **No politician or senior officer ever goes to jail despite huge evidence** because Anti Corruption Branch (ACB) and CBI directly come under the government. Before starting investigation or initiating prosecution in any case, they have to take permission from the same bosses, against whom the case has to be investigated.

System Proposed by Civil Society: Lokpal at centre and Lokayukta at state level will be independent bodies. ACB and CBI will be merged into these bodies. They will have power to initiate investigations and prosecution against any officer or politician without needing anyone's permission. Investigation should be completed within 1 year and trial to get over in next 1 year. **Within two years, the corrupt should go to jail.**

Existing System: **No corrupt officer is dismissed from the job** because Central Vigilance Commission, which is supposed to dismiss corrupt officers, is only an advisory body. Whenever it advises government to dismiss any senior corrupt officer, its advice is never implemented.

System Proposed by Civil Society: Lokpal and Lokayukta will have **complete powers to order dismissal of a corrupt officer.** CVC and all departmental vigilance will be merged into Lokpal and state vigilance will be merged into Lokayukta.

Existing System: **No action is taken against corrupt judges** because permission is required from the Chief Justice of India to even register an FIR against corrupt judges.

System Proposed by Civil Society: Lokpal & Lokayukta shall have **powers to investigate and prosecute any judge** without needing anyone's permission.

Existing System: **Nowhere to go** - People expose corruption but no action is taken on their complaints.

System Proposed by Civil Society: Lokpal & Lokayukta will have to **enquire into and hear every complaint.**

Existing System: **There is so much corruption within CBI and vigilance departments**. Their functioning is so secret that it encourages corruption within these agencies

System Proposed by Civil Society: **All investigations in Lokpal & Lokayukta shall be transparent.** After completion of investigation, all case records shall be open to public. Complaint against any staff of Lokpal & Lokayukta shall be enquired and punishment announced within two months.

Existing System: **Weak and corrupt people are appointed as heads** of anti-corruption agencies.

System Proposed by Civil Society: **Politicians will have absolutely no say in selections** of Chairperson and members of Lokpal & Lokayukta. Selections will take place through a transparent and public participatory process.

Existing System: **Citizens face harassment** in government offices. Sometimes they are forced to pay bribes. One can only complaint to senior officers. No action is taken on complaints because senior officers also get their cut.

System Proposed by Civil Society: Lokpal & Lokayukta will get **public grievances resolved in time bound manner,** impose a penalty of Rs 250 per day of delay to be deducted from the salary of guilty officer and award that amount as compensation to the aggrieved citizen.

Existing System: **Nothing in law to recover ill gotten wealth.** A corrupt person can come out of jail and enjoy that money.

System Proposed by Civil Society: **Loss** caused to the government due to corruption **will be recovered** from all accused.

Existing System: **Small punishment for corruption-** Punishment for corruption is minimum 6 months and maximum 7 years.

System Proposed by Civil Society: **Enhanced punishment -** The punishment would be minimum 5 years and maximum of life imprisonment.

❑

11

Philosophy of Anna

Vivekananda's thoughts gave meaning to his life and he decided to devote the rest of his life working for the society. He read many more books by Vivekananda, Mahatma Gandhi and Acharya Vinoba Bhave. His thoughts started developing and in 1970 he firmly told his parents about his decision not to get married. He urged his parents to go ahead and arrange the marriage of his younger brothers. The new found desire to live beyond his narrow self interest later drove him to seek voluntary retirement from the Army and come back to serve his own village.

Mass support for Anna in his fight against corruption

Following quotes of Anna give glimpse of his working style:

- Over every huge tree that we see over ground, there always is a seed that had submerged itself into the darkness of the soil.
- Ban on consumption and sale of alcohol lays the foundation of rural development.
- It is impossible to change the village without transforming the individual. Similarly it is impossible to transform the country without changing its villages.
- If villages are to develop, politics have to be kept out.
- Education without spirituality cannot help development.
- Money alone does not bring development, but it certainly corrupts.
- In the process of rural development, social and economic development should go hand in hand.
- The work of social transformation is neither easy nor impossible.
- The ultimate goal of all politics and social work should be the upliftment of society and of the nation.
- Books alone cannot prepare future citizens, it requires cultural inputs to do so.
- Educational institutions are not enough to make good citizens, every home should become an educational centre.
- Indulgence causes disease whereas sacrifice leads to accomplishment.

- One should not accept anything free; accepting charity makes one lazy and dependent.
- When the person learns to see beyond his self-interest, he begins to get mental peace.
- One who performs all worldly functions and still remains detached from worldly things is a true saint.
- Salvation of the self is a part of salvation of the people.
- It is experience that gives the direction but it is youth that gives the drive to every plan.

❑

12

Awards to Anna Hazare

- **Padmabhushan**: Presented by R. Venkatraman (President of India) on 6 April 1992 at Delhi for Anna Hazare's social work.
- **Padmashri:** Presented by R. Venkatraman (President of India) on 24 March 1990 at Delhi for Anna Hazare's social work.
- Priyadarshini Vriksha Mitra Award, Govt. of India
- Krushi Bhusahan Govt. of Maharashtra
- Young India Award
- Man of the Year Award 1988
- Sat Paul Mittal National Award 2000 (Nehru Siddhant Kendra Trust Ludhiana, Punjab) on 14 November 2000
- Transparency International (It) Integrity Award 2003 From Transparency International
- Doctorate Degree, Gandhigram Rural Institute--Deemed University Gandhigram Dindigul, Tamil Nadu
- Vivekananda Seva Puraskar 1994, on 12 June 1996 for Anna Hazare's social work done for develop village as a family.

- Shiromani Award 1996, presented by P.A. Sangma (Speaker of Lok Sabha) on 22 February 1997 at New Delhi for Anna Hazare's contribution to National Development Integration, Enrichment of life and for his outstanding achievements in the chosen field of activities (social service).
- Mahaveer Puraskar 1997, presented by Bhagwan Mahaveer Foundation, Chennai on 2 April 1997 for Anna Hazare's excellent in sphere of social & community service.
- Diwaliben Mehta Award, on 8 January 1999 at Mumbai for Anna Hazare's hard, sincere, dedicated and devoted social work.
- Care International Award 1998, presented by Care International Humanitarian on 8 May 1998 at Washington, D.C, USA for Anna Hazare demonstrating a profound commitment to improving life in developing world. Care Recognized Anna Hazare's devotion to the ideas of sustainable development with whole hearted participation of villagers including women & youth.
- Giants International Award, presented by Vilas Rao Deshmukh (Chief Minister of Maharashtra) on 17 September 2000 for Anna Hazare's social work
- Basavshri Prashasti 2000 Award, on 4 June 2000 for Anna Hazare's relentless effort to bring in the value of based way of life in the society.
- National Intergration Award, on 14 February 1999 for Anna Hazare's social work.
- Vishwa-Vatsalya & Santbal Award, presented at Ahmadabad for Anna Hazare's universal services to

mankind including his incessant fight against corruption and his inspiring efforts to improve the living condition of the poor and to raise the ethical levels of the society.

- Jana Seva Puraskar, on 28 February 1998 for Anna Hazare's social work.
- Rotary International Manav Seva Puraskar, presented by Supreme Court Judge Hon. D.P. Wadhwa at India Habital Center, Lodhi Road, New Delhi on 21 Feb 1998 for Anna Hazare's crusade against corruption.

❑

13

Ralegan Siddhi : Model of Environment Conservation

Ralegan Siddhi is a village in Parner taluka of Ahmednagar District, Maharashtra state in western India. It is located at a distance of 87 km from Pune. The village has an area of 982.31 hectares (1991). It is considered a model of environmental conservation. Since 1975, led by the noted social activist Anna Hazare, the village has carried out programs like tree planting, terracing to reduce soil erosion and digging canals to retain rainwater. For energy, the village uses solar power, biogas (some generated from the communal toilet) and a windmill. The project began in 1975, therefore is 36 years old now. It is a sustainable model of a village republic.

The village's biggest accomplishment is in non-conventional energy. For example, all the village streets are lit by solar lights. Each light has a separate solar panel.

The village had 394 households and a population of 2306 in 2001 (male 1265 and female 1041).

In 1975 this same village was caught in a web of poverty and illicit liquor trade. The per capita Income was unbelievably low at Rs. 271. The transformation took place when a retired army driver Anna Hazare settled in the village.

To begin with he donated Rs. 3000 to renovate a local temple. In that temple he baptized the villagers with his five commandments – prohibition, family planning, a ban on open grazing, a ban on felling trees and voluntary labour. Voluntary labour was necessary to ensure minimum dependence on the government for doles. "It socialized the costs of the projects." explains Hazare. Even those who were working outside the village contributed to development by committing a month's salary every year.

A youth group, Tarun Mandal, was formed. The group worked to ban the dowry system, caste discrimination and untouchability. Liquor distilling units were removed and prohibition imposed. Open grazing was completely banned with a new emphasis on stall-feeding. The cultivation of water-intensive crops like sugarcane was banned. Crops such as pulses, oilseeds and certain cash crops with low water requirements were grown.

Anna with a workshop team at Ralegan Siddhi

All elections to local bodies began being held on the basis of consensus. It made the community leaders complete representatives of the people. A system of Nyay Panchayats (Informal courts) was also set up. Since then no case has ever been referred to the police.

A Rs.22 lakhs school building was constructed using only the resources of the village. No money donations were taken. Funds if needed, were borrowed and paid back. The villagers took pride in this self-reliance. A new system of sharing labour grew out of this infusion of pride and voluntary spirit. People volunteered to work on each others' land. Landless labour also gained employment. Today the village plans to buy land for them in adjoining villages.

Today, water is abundant, agriculture flourishes in Ralegan though at a cost the overuse of fertilizers and pesticides. Prosperity also brings to question the ability of the affluent present generation to carry on the work after Anna. The answer lies on Anna's words. "The process of Ralegan's evolution to an ideal village will not stop, with changing times people tend to evolve new ways. In future Ralegan might present a different model to the country.

In the years 1972-73 there was wide spread severe draught in whole of Maharashtra. In order to provide employment to the rural population in this situation Government of Maharashtra decided to undertake soil conservation work in rural areas which required lot of labour. Agriculture and Irrigation Departments of the Government were appointed as nodal agencies to execute the programme and they undertook the work of construction of percolation tanks, nalla bunding and contour bunding in Ralegan Siddhi. While the work was executed in Ralegan Siddhi due to apathy of the Government agencies the percolation tank constructed at Ralegan was not constructed taking due care and was leaking and thus its purpose was defeated.

After his retirement from Army in 1975 he returned to Ralegan Siddhi and was very much disturbed due to condition prevailing there and started discussing with the villagers their problems. He observed that the water problem—both for drinking and irrigation—was acute and felt that something should be done to overcome this problem. At that time he came to know of one Vilasrao Salunkhe who was doing soil and water conservation work at Saswad. He visited the work place of Salunkhe and felt that if similar activity is undertaken at Ralegan Siddhi, the water scarcity problem at Ralegan could be solved. He, therefore, organized villagers meeting (Gram Sabha) to explain to them the work of Mr. Salunkhe and its adoption in Ralegan Siddhi. All the villagers were impressed by this idea and decided to start similar programme in Ralegan Siddhi. Initially they decided to repair the existing percolation tank which was heavily leaking. The cause of seepage of water was ascertained and work of providing core wall by digging puddle trench up to the level of hard rock was undertaken on upper side of the bund through voluntary labour of villagers. Satisfactory completion of the work resulted in retention of water in the tank resulting in recharging of ground water aquifers. This enthused the villagers and they decided to implement the concept of water shed development, *i.e.* ridge to valley approach for soil and water conservation which was hitherto not followed by the Department of Agriculture. Implementation of watershed programme involved lot of expenditure and Anna Hazare approached the then Director of Soil Conservation and requested his help. He had assured the Director that he and his colleagues from village will actively participate in implementation of watershed development programme and will provide labour voluntarily.

The ridge to valley programme involved structures like gully plugging, loose boulder structure, gabion structure, nalla bunding, cement check dams etc. The cost involved in constructing cement check dams was prohibitive and hence Anna Hazare developed modified gabion structure with a core wall which reduced the cost considerably and was as effective as cement check dam. This novel approach is being followed elsewhere also. Similarly on the ridge line where the CCT was not possible, shallow soak pits were dug in order to collect rain water so that through seepage the water would be available to surrounding plantation. This resulted in increase in plant survival and their vigorous growth. This was also a novelty of Ralegan Siddhi programme.

Anna addressing his supporters in his native village

Due to availability of water for irrigation through wells and realizing the importance of water the villagers decided to form cooperative societies well-wise. This resulted in bringing more land under cultivation and developments like double cropping, change of farming system, horticulture plantations, vegetable cultivation, dairy farming etc could take place. It will not be out of place if it is mentioned that from Ralegan Siddhi for some period onions and vegetables were exported to Gulf countries. All this resulted in substantial increase in per capita income of the farmers and the villagers through their cooperative efforts created facilities like school, hostel, gymnasiums, credit societies renovation of temple etc. in the village.

The residents of Ralegan Siddhi are still enjoying the benefits of watershed programme though more than 30 years have passed since completion of programme.

Village Formation Day

In order to foster a sense of unity in the village, the Ralegan Siddhi family celebrated Village annual birthday on 2nd October of every year, on that day…

- The eldest male villager is honoured as father of the village.
- The eldest female villager is honoured as the mother of the village.
- New clothes are stitched for every infant born in the village during the past year, irrespective of the child's cast or religion.
- New brides who have come to the village during the past year are welcomed with the traditional offering of coconut, as they are the daughters-in-law of the village.
- Students who have been successful in education are honoured.
- Youth from the village who have achieved something special are honored.
- All villagers gather in the evening during this occasion and have dinner together to celebrate the event.

❑

14

Bollywood Support for Anna

Bollywood may not be always churning out sensible films, but when it comes to sensible issues, almost the entire industry joins hands, be it the infamous Bharat Shah case, followed by a protest against human trafficking, standing up in unison for the Haiti earthquake victims, 26/11, distributing videos for peace during the Ayodhya verdict earlier this year and so on. This time too, it has expressed solidarity with social activist Anna Hazare on a fast-unto-death on the Lokpal Bill.

Within a day of Anna Hazare began his fast, several joined the campaign through blogs, tweets or press statements. The frenzy has caught up with the seniors and juniors in the industry, right from Aamir Khan, to Hritik Roshan, Shyam Benegal, Farah Khan, Om Puri, Anupam Kher, Raza Murad, Tom Alter, Madhur Bhandarkar, Neetu Chandra, and others. The list goes on.

Usually tight-lipped on anything other than his music, Oscar-winning music director A.R. Rahman spoke on the phone from New Zealand: "The congregation denotes the voice of the people for a corruption-free government/ nation. It is literally the voice of India, which, ultimately, is bound to bring justice to its people." He expressed his happiness that such a mass movement had been started.

Sharmila Tagore was a bit circumspect. "I have great respect for Anna. He has devoted his entire life to social causes and made very important invention in Maharashtra. Now he has chosen corruption, which is at the top of everyone's mind, as for the last one year, week after week, we are hearing of mounting corruption. But I know nothing about Lokpal and Janpal Bills but I am told that both have a lot of problems. So, a fair committee should be formed to first look at these Bills. I am afraid the movement, with the presence of Baba Ram Dev and Shri Shri Ravi Shankar and other brigades, is acquiring a different colour. So, we should not pressure our government, but wait for a healthy outcome."

Anna got strong support from Bollywood also

Actor and filmmaker Aparna Sen viewed the movement with a cool head. "Normally, we select our representative through a voting process and don't get to participate in the law-making activities, and hence, the elements of the bureaucracy remain both the subject and the king. The movement has some credible names such as [dancer] Mallika Sarabhai, [activists] Medha Patkar and Swami Agnivesh, who can be the representatives of civil society in the new law-making decisions."

Ameen Sayani (80), the famous broadcaster who dominated the radio scene for almost four decades, also joined the movement, albeit not physically. "No movement can be a success if it is not supported by a common cause. Since corruption has tested people's patience, it is high time for them to get up and demand justice—not just from the government or sub-government offices but also from the entrepreneurs, industrialists and mafias. It is a necessary campaign which will again test the patience of the people."

Famous singer Shaan and actor of yester-years Padmini Kolhapure too have voiced their support for Anna Hazare.

The young guns of Bollywood are gradually joining the fray and called for immediate drafting of the Bill, ahead of the winter budget and monsoon sessions."The government clearly apprehends that if the civil society is a part of the law-making process, more and more government officers would be exposed. Half the Cabinet would be empty if it denies ticket to netas who have cases against them, so they don't want to face the music," said Shaan.

Although the majority from the industry show unequivocal solidarity to Anna Hazare, some continue to have reservations. Actor Rahul Bose, for instance, is keeping his cool as he absorbs the complexion of the movement. "I am a little confused about the complexion of the campaign. Who are the people who are aligning with it and who are not? I am not a great fan of middle-class radicalism. Of what little I know of the Lokpal and Janpal Bills, neither, in my opinion, are close to being suitable. While one doesn't give enough power to the people, the other goes to the extreme. Neither of them is a balanced mirror to democracy. I would like to know Anna Hazare better before jumping into the campaign in a knee-jerk reaction."

Bollywood on Internet

Bollywood stars Hrithik Roshan and Priyanka Chopra came out in open to support Anna Hazare in his fight against corruption.

Mentioning about it on Twitters, Hrithik wrote, "I support Anna Hazare in his movement. It's Time to make a Change!"

Priyanka also wrote about it on her Twitter account saying, "Just read about Anna Hazare. It's incredible to see the support he has received from across the nation. Also what's remarkable is to see the uprising of the youth of our country in support of Anna Hazare. I pledge my support to this cause started by Anna Hazare."

Shahid Kapoor also pledged support to Anna Hazare. He wrote, "Respect to Anna Hazare for awakening the collective conscience of the country and reminding us there is never a wrong time to do the right"

Vivek Oberai has also supported Anna Hazare. He wrote, "Feeling deeply inspired by Anna Hazare & his incredible commitment to give us a better India, free from the social disease of corruption. Jai Hind"

Many others like Film-maker Farhan Akhtar and actress Sonakshi Sinha have also supported the campaign.

Anupam Kher and Pritish Nandy even joined Anna Hazare at Jantar Mantar, Delhi and spent a night with Anna Hazare and his supporters. Anupam Kher tweeted about Anna Hazare, "It is People's Victory led by a 73 years yougest man in India, Anna Hazare. Thank you for leading us. New journey begins. All the best to us."

Socialite and Film critic Shobha Day tweeted, "If anbody in India deserves a Bharat Ratna it is Anna Hazare. His stadium is India. He bats for every single citizen of this country. Jai Hind!"

Pritish Nandy too wrote on Twitter, "For the first time a new generation of Indians identified with Gandhi and his techniques. While we thought they were outdated!"

He also wrote about atmosphere at Jantar Mantar, where Anna Hazare was sat on fast, "What an electrifying atmosphere at Anna Hazare's fast! Never seen so much joy, hope, excitement on the faces of my fellow Indians."

Actress Bipasha Basu wrote about Anna Hazare, "Anna Hazare is standing up for us, the people of India and he should be supported by us!" She wrote further, "This victory of Anna Hazare shows the strength of people and our democracy! It's a very positive sign for India!" Bipasha Basu wrote again, "Corruption is our enemy and now the tools to fight it will be stronger with the formation of this committee! We need more leaders like Anna Hazare!"

New heartthrob Sonakshi Sinha was not behind. She too claimed her support for Anna Hazare. She too voiced her opinion, "It's usually One person that makes a difference. Mahatma Gandhi, Dalai Lama, Abraham Lincoln, Mother Teresa. Kudos Anna Hazare. We're with you."

Surprisingly nothing was heard from Shahrukh Khan and Javed Akhtar about Anna Hazare. Though Javed Akhtar's wife Shabana Azami along with Urmila Matondkar and Dia Mirza was in Azad Maidan Mumbai to support Anna Hazare. Javed Akhtar's son and director actor Farhan Akhtar says, "I support Anna Hazare. Our country has suffered from corruption for too long. Now is the time we get together and do something about it." Another father- son duo Amitabh Bachchan and Abhishek Bachchan too didn't lend support to Anna Hazare directly.

Gul Panag too went to Jantar Mantar to support Anna Hazare for two days. She posted many pictures on her twitter account too.

❑

15

Anna's Letter to Sonia Gandhi & Sonia Gandhi's Reply to Anna

Social Activist Anna Hazare wrote to UPA Chairperson Sonia Gandhi alleging that a smear campaign has been launched against civil society representatives of the drafting committee of the Lokpal bill. In a strongly worded letter to Sonia Gandhi, Anna pointed to Digvijay Singh and wrote that a general secretary of her party has been making claims regarding the whole campaign which were factually wrong and asked whether she approved of those statements.

Anna's letter to Sonia Gandhi:

To,

Mrs. Sonia Gandhi

Chairperson, NAC & UPA,

10, Janpath, New Delhi

Dear Mrs Sonia Gandhi,

I am really grateful to you for your concern for my health. I am also relieved to note that you fully support the cause and think that 'there is an urgent necessity of combating graft and corruption in public life' and that 'the law in these matters must be effective and deliver the desired results'.

I wish to bring to your notice that the sub-committee of your National Advisory Council (NAC) has agreed with the broad content of Jan Lokpal Bill, barring two issues, after extensive discussions on April 4, 2011 with various knowledgeable sections of society.

May I request you to kindly get the draft discussed at full meeting of NAC at the earliest and recommend the outcome to the government.

I await your early reply.

Warm regards

KB Hazare

Sonia Gandhi's Reply to Anna

Responding to Anna Hazare's complaint against her 'colleagues', Congress President Sonia Gandhi on Wednesday assured him that she does not support 'politics of smear campaign' and that she was strongly committed to the institution of Lokpal.

Writing to Anna Hazare, the chairperson of National Advisory Council, said she believed there was 'urgent necessity' to combat graft and corruption and he should not doubt her commitment in the fight for probity in public life.

She was replying to Anna Hazare's letter in which the social activist said a 'smear' campaign had been launched against civil society members of the joint drafting committee on Lokpal Bill and asked her to advise her 'colleagues' not to try to derail the process of drafting of law.

Sonia's letter to Anna Hazare:

Dear Anna Hazare Ji,

Thank you for your letter of April 18, 2011

Let me reiterate what I wrote to you earlier, that I believe there is an urgent necessity to combat graft and corruption. You should have no doubt of my commitment in the fight for probity in public life. I strongly support the institution of a Lokpal that is consistent with the practices and conventions of our parliamentary democracy.

The Lokpal Bill was very much a part of the agenda of the National Advisory Council.

As you know the NAC Working Group on Transparency, Accountability and Governance under the convenership of Ms Aruna Roy held consultations on this subject on April 4 with several representatives of civil society including Shri Shanti Bhushan, Shri Santosh Hegde and Shri Prashant Bhushan who are now on the joint committee, as well as Swami Agnivesh and Shri Arvind Kejriwal, who have been closely associated with you.

The working group had decided to hold further consultations and evolve broad principles for discussion and approval in the next meeting of the NAC scheduled for April 28.

In fact in your letter of April 8, which my office received at around noon on the date, you yourself said:

"I wish to bring to your notice that the sub-committee of your National Advisory Council (NAC) has agreed with the broad content of Jan Lokpal Bill, barring two issues, after extensive discussions on April 4 with various knowledgeable sections of society.

"May I request you to kindly get the draft discussed at full meeting of NAC at the earliest and recommend the outcome to the government."

As I have just mentioned, this is the very course that the NAC was following until the process was, as you know, overtaken by subsequent events.

As for statements appearing in the media, let me assure you that I do not support nor encourage the politics of smear campaigns.

With good wishes,

Yours sincerely,

Sonia Gandhi

❑

16

Other Social Activists with Anna

Social activists do not belong to any particular professional cult, but they come from all walks of life to bring about some drastic or systematic social changes. These changes concern the transformation of society in relation with social and spiritual upliftment of its inhabitants. India has always been a cradle for social movements and revolutionary decrees.

Many social activists have stepped forward from time to time to question the worth of conventional practices and to light up the darkened corridors of ignorance that typify Indian society in many ways.

During the Anna's campaign against corruption many social activists lent their support. Brief life sketch of some of the activists are as follows:

Kiran Bedi

Anna Hazare's close aide and former 'super cop' Kiran Bedi is of the view that anti-corruption movement has just begun, and gives full credit to the youth and people of India who made it 'their' movement.

Kiran Bedi is truly an icon of heroism. She was the first Indian woman to join the Indian Police Services. She was born on June 9, 1949 at Amritsar in Punjab. She is one of the most renowned police officers, who have put in their whole hearted effort in serving the society.

She served as the Director General of India's Bureau of Police Research and Development. Earlier, she served as the Police Advisor in the United Nations peacekeeping department. For her noteworthy performance, she was awarded with the UN medal. In the year 2005, she received the honorary degree of Doctor of Law.

She did her schooling from the Sacred Heart Convent School in Amritsar. She completed her graduation in the English language from the Government College for Women in Amritsar. She received her Master's degree in Political Science from Punjab University, Chandigarh. She continued her studies, even when she joined the Indian Police force. In the year 1988, she obtained a degree in Law (LLB) from Delhi University.

Kiran Bedi with Anna Hazare showing Gazzete Notification

In the year 1993, the Department of Social Sciences, the Indian Institute of Technology in New Delhi awarded her with a Ph.D. degree. Her topic of research was Drug Abuse and Domestic Violence. Kiran Bedi has won the championship of all-India and all-Asian tennis competition. When she was 22 years old, she won the Asian Women Title.

Her career started in the year 1970, when she took the job of a lecturer at Khalsa College for Women in Amritsar. Two years later, she joined the Indian Police Services. All the way through her career, she has taken up a number of challenging assignments. She has served as the Traffic Commissioner of New Delhi, Deputy Inspector General of Police in the insurgency prone area of Mizoram.

She has also been the Lieutenant Governor of Chandigarh and Director General of Narcotics Control Bureau. An interesting thing about Kiran Bedi is that, sometimes, she is referred to as Crane Bedi. The reason behind calling her by this name is that, she dragged the car of Prime Minister Indira Gandhi due to violation of parking rules.

Kiran Bedi made the Indian Police Service change its decision in matters related to traffic management, control over narcotics and VIP security. During her tenure as the Inspector General of Tihar Jail, she brought about several reforms in the way the prisons are managed. She brought forth a number of measures like yoga, meditation, redressal of complaints made by the prisoners etc.

Kiran Bedi laid the foundation for the establishment of two voluntary organizations, namely, Navajyoti (1988) & India Vision Foundation (1994). These organizations were primarily set up with the aim of improving the living conditions of the drug addicts and the underprivileged people. The effort of Kiran Bedi has paid and brought her worldwide recognition. Her works have always earned appreciation. For drug abuse prevention, her organization was presented with the Serge Soitiroff Memorial Award by the United Nations.

Kiran Bedi said in an interview that, "I am truly blessed to be a part of a movement to save my country from the clutches of the dishonest high and mighty. With Anna Hazare in the lead we were sure to achieve a breakthrough. However it's just the beginning. And long way to go with Herculean challenges. But I am so grateful to the Almighty that it has become a national reform movement."

Swami Agnivesh

This unusual swami has been consistently doing battles on behalf of the poor, the weak and the defenseless of India. Agnivesh's campaigns have led him to fight alcoholism, female foeticide, bonded labour, child labour as well as struggle for the emancipation of women.

He looks like a sadhu, talks like a politician and most importantly voices the case of the underprivileged millions of India. Swami Agnivesh is a strange man by all counts. He puzzles and provokes at once, and is loved by the masses.

Unlike the politicians who mouth religion between the teeth of communalism, Agnivesh participates in politics as an outworking of his spirituality. He bridges politics and religion with the plank of social justice. In a way parallel to the liberation theologians of Latin America, the swami has been waging war relentlessly on behalf of the poor, the weak and the defenceless of India.

He preaches. But preaches only what he practices. His words catch fire in the heat of his involvement imprinted with the zeal of compassion. He leads and inspires. His date with the oppressed and passion for social justice are as old as his political career which goes back many years to his entry into the Haryana Assembly in 1977.

'My saffron garb,' you will hear Swamiji say, *'is my uniform for socio-spiritual action, a call to battle on behalf of the oppressed.'* Saffron is the colour of sacrifice, commitment and purity and he believes it helps him in his work of love, truth, compassion and justice. He says with utmost realism: "If my clothes come in the way of this, I won't mind renouncing them. It matters little if you call me "Swami Agnivesh" or simply "Agnivesh". All that matters is that the fire inside of me, the presence of the divine in the inner temple of my being, should continue to blaze till the end.

Baba Ramdev & Swami Agnivesh with Anna Hazare

He narrates a tale of how during a visit to the island of Mindanao in the Philippines to be with the rebels encamped there, he was told that his saffron garb would make him highly conspicuous. 'Then, I quickly switched over to jeans and a T-shirt,' he says.

Swami Agnivesh is easily the most distinguished leader of the Arya Samaj. He was appointed the Chairperson of the UN Trust Fund on Contemporary Forms of Slavery. He is better known across India for his campaigns against bonded labour, and is founder-head of the Bandhu Mukti Morcha (Bonded Labour Liberation Front). He has been appointed the President of the World Council of Arya Samaj (Sarvadeshik Arya Pratinidhi Sabha).

So far, his campaigns have led him to fight against alcoholism, female foeticide, bonded labour, child labour, and for the emancipation of women. His current 'mission' includes fighting the consumer culture and the Western model of development in India, opposing Western cultural imperialism, and battling casteism, obscurantism and communalism.

Arvind Kejriwal

Arvind Kejriwal is a social activist for greater transparency in Government. He was awarded Ramon Magsaysay Award for Emergent Leadership in 2006, for activating India's Right to Information movement at grassroots and social activities to empower the poorest citizens to fight corruption by holding the government answerable to the people.

Arvind Kejriwal was born in Hissar, Haryana in 1968, and graduated from IIT Kharagpur as a Mechanical engineer in 1989. Later, he joined the Indian Revenue Service (IRS), a part of the Indian Civil Services in 1992, and was posted at the Income-tax Commissioner's Office in Delhi. Soon, he realized that much of the corruption prevalent in government is owing to lack of transparency in the process. Even while in his official position, he started crusading against the corrupt practices. Initially, Arvind was instrumental in bringing in a number of changes to increase transparency in the Income Tax office.

From L. to R.—Arvind Kejriwal, Anna Hazare, Kiran Bedi & Swami Agnivesh

In January 2000, he took a sabbatical from work and founded *Parivartan* – a Delhi based citizens' movement which works on ensuring just, transparent and accountable governance. Thereafter, in February 2006, he resigned from the job, to work full-time at *Parivartan*.

Together with Aruna Roy and others, he campaigned for the Right to Information Act, which soon became a silent social movement. Delhi Right to Information Act was passed in 2001 and eventually at the national-level Act the Indian Parliament passed the Right to Information Act (RTI) in 2005. Thereafter, in July 2006, he spearheaded an awareness campaign for RTI across India. To motivate others Arvind has now instituted an RTI Award through his organisation.

The right to information holds as much importance in the lives of the poor as it does for the general public and professionals. Yet, many Indians remain passive spectators in the process of electing governments. Arvind uses the Right to Information Act to equip individual citizens with the power to question their government. Through his organization *Parivartan* he promotes participation in governance by people.

On February 6, 2007, Arvind was named CNN-IBN 'Indian of the Year' in Public Service for the year 2006.

As a member of India against Corruption he is a active participant in the movement for the enactment of Jan Lokpal Bill in April 2011.

Shanti Bhushan

Born on 11 November 1925 Shanti Bhushan is a former Law Minister of India at Ministry of Law and Justice (1977–1979) in the Morarji Desai Ministry and also a senior advocate. He along with his son Prashant Bhushan was featured at 74th position in a list of the most powerful Indians published by The Indian Express in 2009.

Shanti Bhushan &
his son Prashant Bhushan

Shanti Bhushan was an active member of Congress (O) party and later the Janata Party. He was a member of the Rajya Sabha from 14 July 1977 to 2 April 1980 and the Union Law minister in the Morarji Desai ministry from 1977 to 1979. He joined the Bhartiya Janata Party in 1980. In 1986, he resigned from BJP after the party acted against his advice over an election petition.

Shanti Bhushan then as the Law Minister had introduced Lokpal bill in 1977, but it could never see the light of the day, because of the collapse of the government.

Shanti Bhushan, along with his son Prashant Bhushan has been involved in accountability of the Indian Judiciary by setting up Campaign for Judicial Accountability and Judicial Reform (CJAR).

The father son duo are currently facing contempt of court at Supreme Court of India for their statement about corruption in higher judiciary specifically, former chief justices of Supreme Court.

Justice Santosh Hegde

Hon. Nitte Santosh Hegde is a former justice of the Supreme Court Of India, former Solicitor General of India and the present Lokayukta for Karnataka State of India.

Santosh Hegde was born on 16 June 1940 in Udupi district in Karnataka to former speaker of Lok Sabha, Justice K.S.

Hegde and his wife Meenakshi Hegde. He had his early education at St. Aloysius College, Mangalore and Madras Christian College in Madras. He completed his intermediate from St. Joseph's College, Bangalore and B.Sc. from Central College of Bangalore. Santosh Hegde graduated with a law degree from Government Law College (now known as University Law College), Bangalore in 1965.

Hon. Retired Justice Santosh Hegde
– The architect of Jan Lokpal Bill

After completing apprenticeship training, he enrolled as an advocate in January 1966 and was designated as senior advocate in May 1984. Hegde was appointed as the Advocate General for the state of Karnataka in February 1984 and held that position till August 1988. He worked as additional Solicitor General of India from December 1989 to November 1990 and was re-appointed as the Solicitor General of India on April 25, 1998.

Santosh Hegde was appointed as a judge of Supreme Court of India on January 8, 1999. He retired as judge of Supreme Court of India in June 2005. He was conferred honorary doctorate of law degree by Mangalore University in 2005 A.D. For a brief period he worked as Chairperson of Telecom Dispute Settlement Appellate Tribunal, New Delhi.

Hegde was of the view that Telecom Regulatory Authority of India (TRAI) was not the authority for dispute resolution between customers and telecommunication service providers.

Aruna Roy

Aruna Roy was born in Chennai, and was an IAS officer until 1974. She resigned from the IAS to join the Social Work and Research Center in Tilonia, Rajasthan, which had been set up by her husband Sanjit Roy. She worked at the SWRC until 1983, then moved to Devdoondri in 1990 and set up the Mazdoor Kisan Shakti Sangathana, a group which is a working example of a transparent organization. She is a strong supporter of the movement for Right to Information, which succeeded in getting the Rajasthan Right to Information Bill passed.

The MKSS built a grassroots movement that has triggered broad debate and a nationwide demand for the public's right to scrutinize official records—a crucial check against arbitrary governance.

In 2000, she was awarded the Ramon Magsaysay award for Community Leadership and International Understanding, along with J. Arputham, the President of the National Slumdwellers' Federation. Aruna Roy requested that the award be given to the Mazdoor Kisan Shakti Sangathana, but was informed that it was only given to individuals. She put the award money into a trust to support the process of democratic struggles.

❑

17

Transformation of Anna's Native Village

After voluntary retirement from the army, Anna Hazare went to Ralegan Siddhi village in 1975. Initially he organised the youth of the village into an organisation named the *Tarun Mandal* (Youth Association). He helped to form the *Pani Puravatha Mandals* (Water Supply Associations) to ensure proper distribution of water.

Watershed Development Programme

Ralegan is located in the foothills, so Anna Hazare persuaded villagers to construct a watershed embankment to stop water and allow it to percolate and increase the ground water level and improve irrigation in the area. Residents of the village used *shramdan* (voluntary labour) to build canals, small-scale check-dams, and percolation tanks in the nearby hills for watershed development. These efforts solved the problem of water scarcity of water in the village and made irrigation possible. The first embankment that was built using volunteer efforts developed a leak and had to be reconstructed, this time with government funding.

In order to conserve soil and water by checking runoff, contour trenches and gully plugs were constructed along the hill slopes. Grass, shrubs and about 3 lakh trees were planted along the hillside and the village. This process was supplemented by afforestation, *nullah bunds*, underground check dams, and cemented *bandharas* (small diversion weirs) at strategic locations. Ralegan has also experimented with drip and bi-valve irrigation. Papaya, lemon, and chillies have been planted on a plot of 80 acres entirely irrigated by the drip irrigation system. Cultivation of water-intensive crops like sugar cane was banned. Crops such as pulses, oilseeds, and certain cash crops with low water requirements were grown. The farmers started growing high-yield varieties of crop and the cropping pattern of the village was changed. Anna Hazare has helped farmers of more than 70 villages in drought-prone regions in the state of Maharashtra since 1975.

The Government of India plans to start a training centre in Ralegan Siddhi to understand and implement Anna Hazare's watershed development model in other villages in the country.

Education

In 1932 Ralegan Siddhi got its first formal school, a single classroom primary school. In 1962 the villagers added more classrooms through community volunteer efforts. By 1971, out of an estimated population of 1,209, only 30.43% were literate (72 women and 290 men). Boys moved to the nearby towns of Shirur and Parner to pursue higher education, but due to socio-economic conditions, girls could not do the same and were limited to primary education. Anna Hazare, along with the youth of Ralegan Siddhi, worked to increase literacy rates and education levels. In 1976 they started a pre-school and a high school in 1979. The villagers formed a charitable trust, the *Sant Yadavbaba Shikshan Prasarak Mandal*, which was registered in 1979.

The trust obtained a government grant of Rs. 4 lakhs for the school building using the National Rural Education Programme. This money funded a new school building that was built over the next two months using volunteer labour.

A new hostel was constructed to house 200 students from poorer sections of society. After the opening of the school, a girl from Ralegan Siddhi became the first female in the village to complete her Secondary School Certificate in 1982. Since then the school has been instrumental in bringing in many of changes to the village. Traditional farming practices are taught in this school in addition to the government curriculum.

Against Alcoholism

Anna Hazare and the youth group next decided to take up the issue of alcoholism. At a meeting conducted in the temple, the villagers resolved to close down liquor dens and ban alcohol in the village. Since these resolutions were made in the temple, they became in a sense religious commitments. Over thirty liquor brewing units were closed by their owners voluntarily. Those who did not succumb to social pressure were forced to close down their businesses when the youth group smashed up their liquor dens. The owners could not complain as their businesses were illegal.

Some villagers continued to drink in Ralegan Siddhi, as they obtained their liquor from neighbouring villages. The villagers decided that those men would be given three warnings, after which they would be physically punished. Twelve men who were found in a drunken state after warnings were tied to a pole with help from the youth group and flogged. Anna Hazare said, "Doesn't a mother administer bitter medicines to a sick child when she knows that the medicine can cure her child? The child may not like the medicine, but the mother does it only because she cares for the child. The alcoholics were punished so that their families would not be destroyed."

Anna Hazare appealed to the government of Maharashtra to bring in a law whereby prohibition would come into force in a village if 25% of the women in the village demanded it. In July 2009 the state government issued a government resolution amending the Bombay Prohibition Act, 1949. As per the amendments, if at least 25% of women voters demand liquor prohibition through a written application to the state excise department, voting should be conducted through a secret ballot. If 50% of the voters vote against the sale of liquor, prohibition should be imposed in the village and the sale of liquor should be stopped. Similar action can be taken at the ward level in municipal areas. Another circular was issued making it mandatory to get the sanction of the Gram Sabha (the local self government) for issuing new permits for the sale of liquor. In some instances, when women agitated against the sale of liquor, cases were filed against them. Anna Hazare took up the issue again. In August 2009 the government issued another circular that sought withdrawal of cases against women who sought prohibition of liquor in their villages.

It was decided to ban the sale of tobacco, cigarettes, and beedies (a speciality cigarette) in the village. In order to implement this resolution, the youth group performed a unique 'Holi' ceremony twenty two years ago. The festival of Holi is celebrated as a symbolic burning of evil. The youth group brought all the tobacco, cigarettes, and beedies from the shops in the village and burnt them in a 'Holi' fire. Tobacco, cigarettes, or beedies are no longer sold in any shops at Ralegan Siddhi.

Collective Marriages

Most rural poor get into a debt trap as they incur heavy expenses at the time of marriage of their son or daughter. It is an undesirable practice but has almost become a social obligation in India. Ralegan's people have started celebrating marriages collectively. Joint feasts are held, where the expenses are further reduced by the *Tarun Mandal* taking responsibility for cooking and serving the food. The vessels, the loudspeaker system, the mandap, and the decorations have also been bought by the *Tarun Mandal* members belonging to the oppressed castes. From 1976 to 1986, 424 marriages have been held under this system.

Gram Sabha

The Gandhian philosophy on rural development considers the Gram Sabha as an important democratic institution for collective decision making in the villages of India. Anna Hazare campaigned between 1998 and 2006 for amending the Gram Sabha Act, so that the villagers have a say in the development works in their village. The state government initially refused, but eventually gave in due to public pressure. As per the amendments, it is mandatory to seek the sanction of the Gram Sabha (an assembly of all village adults, and not just the few elected representatives in the gram panchayat) for expenditures on development works in the village. In case of expenditure without the sanction of the Gram Sabha, 20% of Gram Sabha members can lodge a complaint to the Chief Executive Officer of the zila parishad (the district-level governing body) with their signatures. The Chief Executive Officer is required to visit the village and conduct an inquiry within 30 days and submit a report to the divisional commissioner, who has the power to remove the sarpanch or deputy sarpanch and dismiss the gram sevak involved. Anna Hazare was not satisfied as the amended Act did not include the right to recall a sarpanch. He insisted that this should be included and the state government relented.

In Ralegan Siddhi, Gram Sabha meetings are held periodically to discuss issues relating to the welfare of the village. Projects like watershed development activities are undertaken only after they are discussed in the Gram Sabha. All decisions like *Nashabandi* (bans on alcohol), *Kurhadbandi* (bans on tree felling), *Charai bandi* (bans on grazing), and *Shramdan* were taken in the Gram Sabha. Decisions are taken in a simple majority consensus. The decision of the Gram Sabha is accepted as final.

In addition to the panchayat, there are several registered societies that take care of various projects and activities of the village. Each society presents an annual report and statement of accounts in the Gram Sabha. The *Sant Yadavbaba Shikshan Prasarak Mandal* monitors the educational activities. The *Vividh Karyakari Society* gives assistance and provides guidance to farmers regarding fertilizers, seeds, organic farming, and financial assistance. The *Sri Sant Yadavbaba Doodh Utpadhak Sahakari Sanstha* gives guidance regarding the dairy business. Seven co-operative irrigation societies provide water to the farmers from cooperative wells. The *Mahila Sarvage Utkarsh Mandal* attends the welfare needs of women.

Removal of Untouchability

The social barriers and discrimination that existed due to the caste system in India have been largely eliminated by Ralegan Siddhi villagers. People of all castes come together to celebrate social events. The Dalits have been integrated into the social and economic life of the village. The villagers have built houses for the Dalits, and helped to repay their loans to free them from their indebtedness.

Milk Production

As a secondary occupation, milk production was promoted in Ralegan Siddhi. Purchase of new cattle and improvement of the existing breed with the help of artificial insemination and timely guidance and assistance by a veterinarian resulted in an improvement in the cattle stock. Milk production has increased. Crossbred cows are replacing local ones which gave a lower milk yield. The number of milk cattle has also been growing, which resulted in growth from 100 litres (before 1975) to around 2,500 litres per day. The milk is sent to a co-operative dairy (Malganga Dairy) in Ahmednagar. Some milk is given to *Balwadi* (kindergarten) children and neighbouring villages under the child nutrition program sponsored by the Zila Parishad.

From the surplus funds generated, the milk society bought a mini-truck and a thresher. The mini-truck is used to transport milk to Ahmednagar and to take vegetables and other produce directly to the market, thus eliminating intermediate agents. The thresher is rented out to farmers during the harvesting season.

❑

18

Civil Society Members Declared Their Assets

Ahead of first meeting of the joint committee to draft the anti-graft Lokpal Bill, civil society members on the panel declared their assets.

- Social activist Anna Hazare, who went on a 97-hour fast that led the government to set up the joint panel, submitted that he owns 2.53 hectares land, valued at Rs.68,688.36. Out of this, 0.07 hectares is family land being used by other family members, 2 hectares donated by the army was in turn donated for his village's use and 0.46 hectares, donated by villagers to Hazare, was also donated for common use. He has a balance of 67,188.36 in his bank account and Rs.1,500 cash in hand.
- Shanti Bhushan submitted a statement of account at Rs.1,367,172,287 for the last ten years. He revealed he owns three houses and two flats in Noida, a plot in Banglore, a house in Allahabad, agricultural land in Roorkee (Uttarakhand) and farmland in Noida measuring 10,000 square meters.
- His son, Prashant Bhushan owns a house in Jangpura area of New Delhi, a flat in Supreme Cooperative

Group Housing Society, 4,800 square metres agriculture land in Himanchal Pradesh, a share in a housing property in Allahabad and movable property valued at Rs.2 crore.

- Justice Hegde, presently the Lok Ayukta (Ombudsman) of Karnataka, declared he has cash amounting to Rs. 30,00,000 in three bank accounts in State Bank of India and Yes Bank.
- Arvind Kejriwal declared his properties to be worth Rs.55 lakh.

❑

www.ingramcontent.com/pod-product-compliance
Lightning Source LLC
LaVergne TN
LVHW010109170826
845678LV00012B/2309